LOCOMOTION PAPERS

The Winsford & Over Branch

by
R.W. Miller

THE OAKWOOD PRESS

British Library Cataloguing in Publication Data
A Record for this book is available from the British Library
ISBN 0 85361 546 2

Typeset by Oakwood Graphics.
Repro by Ford Graphics, Ringwood, Hants.
Printed by The Witney Press, Witney, Oxon.

Even as late as June 1955 passengers arriving at Cuddington were still being invited to change for Whitegate and Winsford (but not Over), despite there having been no trains on the branch for over 24 years. The nameboard had been shortened to just CUDDINGTON by 1959. *Author*

Title page: Seen at Over Fair *c.* 1907, CLC horse and 'lurry' No. 29. The name of the horse is not recorded but the rider might well be Teddy. Note the beautifully polished brasses whilst among the shrubbery on the 'lurry' there is a model railway complete with signal, locomotive and four coaches. *Gordon Whitehead, via Trevor Booth*

Published by The Oakwood Press (Usk), P.O. Box 13, Usk, Mon., NP15 1YS.

E-Mail: oakwood-press@dial.pipex.com
Website: http://ds.dial.pipex.com/oakwood-press

Contents

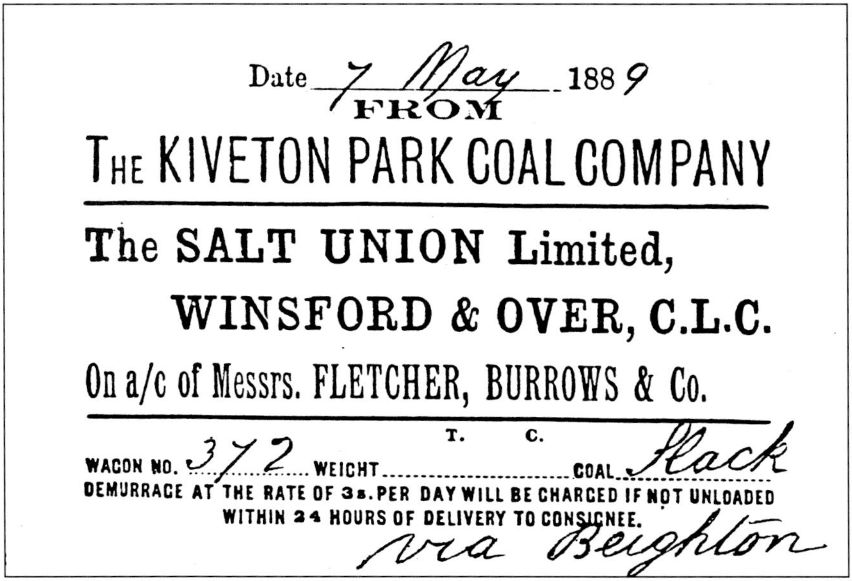

Date 7 May 1889
FROM

THE KIVETON PARK COAL COMPANY

The SALT UNION Limited,

WINSFORD & OVER, C.L.C.

On a/c of Messrs. FLETCHER, BURROWS & Co.

T.   C.

WAGON NO. 372 WEIGHT................. COAL Slack

DEMURRAGE AT THE RATE OF 3s. PER DAY WILL BE CHARGED IF NOT UNLOADED
WITHIN 24 HOURS OF DELIVERY TO CONSIGNEE.

via Beighton

A wagon label for a consignment to Winsford in 1889.

3

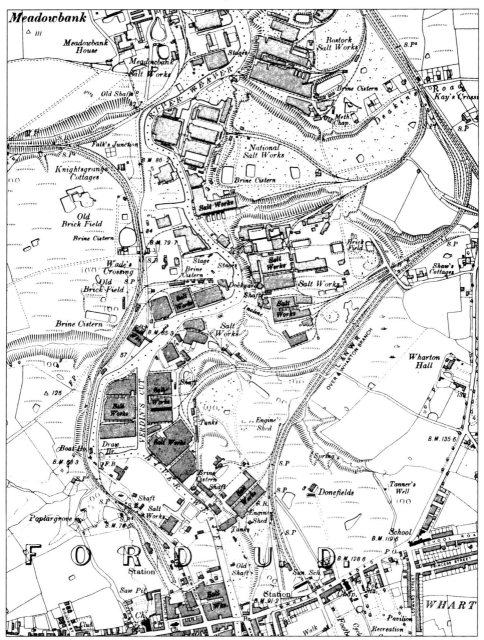

The 1911 6 in. Ordnance Survey map of Winsford showing the close proximity of the CLC's Winsford & Over station and the LNWR's Over & Wharton branch.

Chapter One

A Branch Line to Winsford

The longest and most individual of several short branch lines operated by the Cheshire Lines Committee (CLC) was that from Cuddington to Winsford and Over, slightly more than six miles in length. Opened in 1870 it enjoyed a distinctly chequered career. Passengers were originally considered a nuisance as they interfered with the real purpose of the line, to serve the numerous salt works on the west bank of the River Weaver. Twice the branch was closed to passengers but services were reinstated after a few years, the second time only after the CLC had been taken to the Royal Courts of Justice. The third and final withdrawal occurred in 1931 and again the CLC was taken to court, but this time it won its case and the branch reverted to goods traffic only until complete closure in 1967. Most of the route was single line but at one time the final mile into Winsford was double track with the curiosity that all passenger trains used only the up line. Today, much of the trackbed has been purchased by the County Council and converted into a public footpath and bridleway, with a visitor centre established at the one intermediate station at Whitegate.

The town of Winsford lies on the River Weaver (the ford having been replaced by a bridge as early as the 14th century) in the very heart of Cheshire; an oak tree in the grounds of Bostock Hall, hard by the junction of the A533 and A5013 roads just 1½ miles north-east of Winsford, is reputed to be the exact centre of the old county. Winsford was, of course, one of the Cheshire salt towns, but industrialisation only really took off after the Weaver was made navigable in 1732, most of the expansion taking place from the 1840s to the 1880s. A number of foreign workers were brought in and this, together with the insanitary conditions of the time, was blamed for the last cholera epidemic to hit Cheshire, at Winsford in 1865.

By the 1890s there were over 2,000 men employed in the town's salt works, with 600 open pans in production, nearly all lining both banks of the river for more than a mile northwards from Winsford Bridge. The decline in the traditional method of making salt by heating brine in pans, which could be up to 140 ft by 30 ft in size, started as early as 1905 and accelerated in the 1930s, with the last open pan works closing in 1961. Today the only salt produced in Winsford is extracted by mining, and distribution is entirely by road transport. Salt now forms only a very minor part of Winsford's economy.

As the town grew, reaching a population of around 12,000 at the turn of the century (1901), it encompassed the neighbouring villages of Over a mile to the west, and Wharton which is a half-mile to the north-east. However growth since 1900 has been slow, only reaching 14,120 in the 1961 census. The big developments took place during the next 20 years when Winsford nearly doubled in size to 26,941 in 1981, but this was too late to be of any benefit to the Cheshire Lines.

The first railway in the area was the Grand Junction, opened in 1837 and a constituent of the London & North Western Railway (LNWR) on its formation in 1846. Winsford station was a mile to the south-east of the town, and was known to Winsfordians as the Gravel station, the old name of Station Road being Gravel Lane. In LNWR days, mostly in the 1860s, a series of branch lines were constructed down to the salt works on the east side of the river. The salt works on the opposite bank had to wait until 1870 to be rail connected, when the Cheshire Lines opened its own branch to a terminal near the town centre which it called Winsford and Over. Some 12 years later the LNWR extended its southernmost salt branch to its own passenger and goods terminus and gave this the name Over and Wharton. Now, like the CLC, all these branches on the LNWR side of the Weaver have gone, the last in 1982, and the original Grand Junction line is the only one left in Winsford. The Gravel station is still in use, for passengers only, albeit completely rebuilt in the modern idiom.

The Winsford and Over branch had its origins in the proposals of the West Cheshire Railway (WCR), which was promoted in 1860 to extend the Cheshire Midland Railway (then under construction to Northwich) through to Chester with a branch to Helsby. A Bill was presented to Parliament in 1861 which for the moment did not include the proposed branch to Winsford. Parliament threw out the Mouldsworth to Chester section but approved the rest of the route, so the Northwich-Mouldsworth-Helsby line was authorised by an Act of 11th July, 1861 (Vict. 24/5, cap. 143) with a capital of £200,000 in £10 shares, to which the Great Northern and the Manchester, Sheffield & Lincolnshire (MS&L) Railways could each subscribe up to a maximum of £65,000, together with loans of £66,600. The Cheshire Midland (CMR) was conceived as a prolongation of the Manchester, South Junction & Altrincham Railway, in which the MS&L and LNWR had an equal share. However the LNWR decided to approach Knutsford with its own line from Chelford (authorised on 28th June, 1861 but never built) and Northwich from Sandbach (authorised 21st July, 1863 and opened on 11th November, 1867) so declined to invest in the Cheshire Midland. Accordingly the MS&L invited the Great Northern (GNR) to take the place of the LNWR as partner in the venture, to which the new partners contributed much of the required capital and agreed to work the line on completion. The first part of the Cheshire Midland opened to traffic on 12th May, 1862.

That year the WCR was back in Parliament with another Bill, and again the Mouldsworth to Chester section was rejected, but sanction was given for a branch to Winsford and another from Hartford to Winnington, together with a deviation at Oakmere on the main line, for which additional capital of £63,000 plus loans of £21,000 were allowed. This received the Royal Assent on 29th July, 1862 (Vict. 25/6, cap. 190). Powers were given for the WCR to enter into agreements with the MS&L and GNR and for them to work the line jointly on completion.

The Parliamentary plans for the Winsford branch were deposited in the office of the Clerk of the Peace for Cheshire at 5.50 pm on Friday 29th November, 1861. The route was 5 miles 23 chains* long and commenced a little west of Cuddington station by a junction with the main line facing towards Mouldsworth. From just beyond the crossing of the Cuddington to Over road, by Marton Hall, the authorised route continued in a straight line for nearly two miles to a terminus on the west bank of the Weaver at the southern end of the Meadowbank Salt Works, one mile north of Winsford Bridge.

---

* 1 chain = 22 yards, 80 chains = 1 mile.

The GN and MS&L railways signed an agreement on 11th June, 1862 to form a joint committee to work the WCR, CMR, and also two other lines in Cheshire when they were completed, and this agreement was ratified by Parliament by the Act of 13th July, 1863 (Vict. 26/7, cap. 147) which thus made this Cheshire Lines Committee, as the joint committee was named, a legal entity. The West Cheshire ceased to exist as an independent railway with the passing of the Cheshire Lines Transfer Act on 5th July, 1865 (Vict. 28/9, cap. 327) which vested the WCR and the CMR in the CLC. The same Act empowered the Midland Railway to buy a third share in the CLC, and this they completed on 18th July, 1866. From this date the CLC was composed of nine committee members, being the Chairman and two other Directors appointed from the three Boards of the GN, the Midland, and the MS&L railways. There was no regular Chairman of the CLC, members taking turns by rotation to chair meetings.

Before being taken over by the CLC in 1865 the West Cheshire Railway had a Board of eight Directors, six being the Chairmen and two other Directors each from the GN and MS&L railways, leaving two to represent the ordinary shareholders - Sir Harry Mainwaring of Peover Hall, who was the WCR Chairman, and Henry Long of Knutsford. Edward Ross of the MS&L was Secretary, John Isaac Mawson the Engineer and Robert William Bennett of Manchester the Solicitor.

Matrix seal of the West Cheshire Railway, with the Arms of Birkenhead on the left and Cheshire on the right.   *Author's Collection*

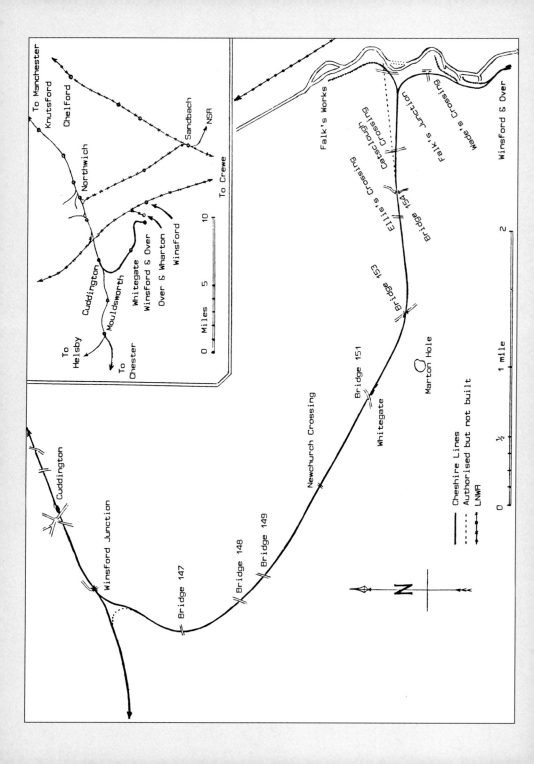

Chapter Two

The Route and Gradients

For much of its life most of the branch trains, both passenger and goods, terminated their journeys at Cuddington, on the CLC main line between Manchester Central and Chester Northgate. The small town of Cuddington (population in 1981: 5,573), famous for its Cheshire cheeses, was not the destination for most passengers; they preferred to change trains and carry on another five miles to the much larger town of Northwich (population 1901: 17,609; and in 1981 little changed at 17,195) or to continue on to Manchester. The branch trains were generally timed to connect with the Manchester services but were not as convenient if passengers wished to travel in the other direction towards Chester.

Surprisingly, Cuddington station was not provided with a bay platform for the local services, the original intention being to terminate these at Northwich. After unloading, branch trains had to continue another ¼ mile on the main line before backing into either the up siding or, more usually, one of the two down sidings before the engine could run round. It then had to wait for the down (Chester bound) main line train to clear the platform before drawing the branch train forward for loading for Whitegate and Winsford. Cuddington then just had the two platforms with the main buildings and the station master's house on the up side. These were a standard WCR design, being brick built like Hartford, whereas Delamere and Mouldsworth station buildings were of sandstone. Cuddington signal box, of all-timber construction, stood at the Northwich end of the up platform. The simple goods facilities were enlarged about 1900 with an extra siding and a goods shed, and the up siding was lengthened. Outside the station, on Warrington Road, is a row of four CLC cottages for signalmen and station staff; these are believed to date from 1886. The line through the station is on a grade of 1 in 300 rising towards Chester, but just beyond the station alters to fall at 1 in 125 as far as Winsford Junction.

As eventually built, the Winsford branch showed several departures from the route authorised by Parliament and depicted on the deposited plans. The branch commenced 52 chains west of Cuddington station with a junction facing towards Northwich, whereas the Parliamentary route showed a trailing junction here. The alteration seems to have been effected mostly within the limits of deviation allowed to both the branch and main line. The Junction signal box was on the up side, and behind it were a pair of signalmen's cottages. Like the similar cottages at Mouldsworth and formerly at Delamere, these are of an earlier pattern than those at Cuddington, and probably date from 1870. The double junction quickly changed to single track as the Winsford line, climbing sharply at 1 in 82, struck off to the south-west to enter Delamere Forest and run alongside Lobstock Wood, in the grounds of Oakmere Hall, and pass under the main Northwich to Chester road (A556) after 54 chains by bridge No. 147. The gradient eases slightly to 1 in 127 rising as the branch curves round to the south-east and enters a deep cutting, passing under Bridge No. 148 which carries the

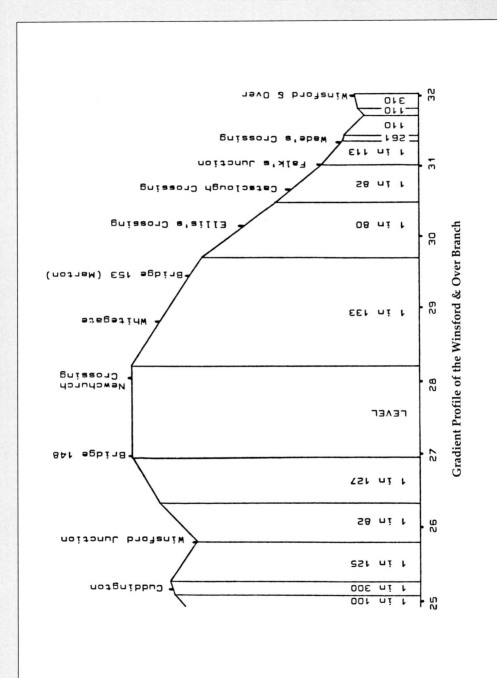

Gradient Profile of the Winsford & Over Branch

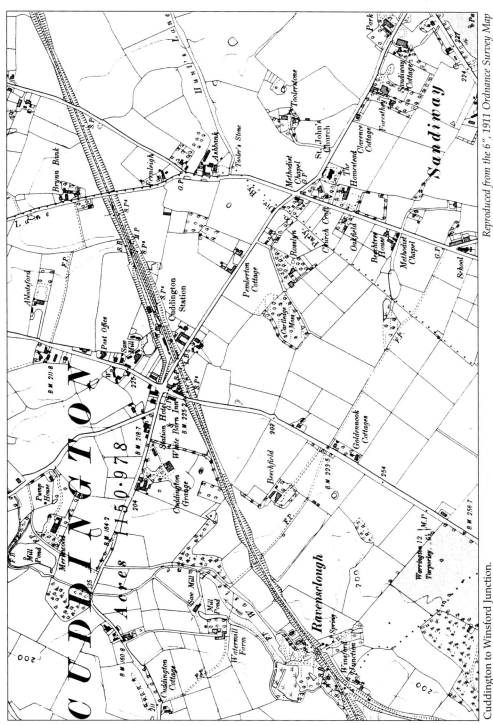

Reproduced from the 6", 1911 Ordnance Survey Map

Cuddington to Winsford Junction.

A view of Cuddington looking towards Northwich in 1961, showing the goods shed and signal box.   *Author*

The station buildings on the up (Northwich bound) platform at Cuddington in August 1970.
                                                                                                 Author

The station buildings on the up (Northwich bound) platform at Cuddington in 1952.
L&GRP 26332

A row of four railwaymen's cottages at Cuddington, of the second CLC standard design, dating from about 1886, photographed in September 1980.
Author

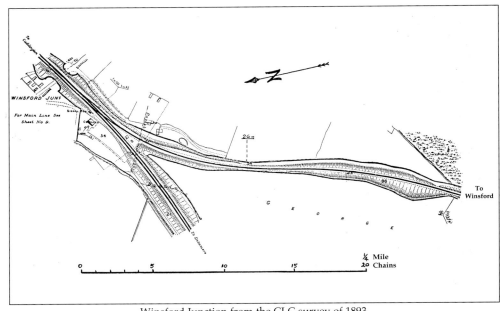

Winsford Junction from the CLC survey of 1893.

The pair of signalmen's cottages on the north side of the line at Winsford Junction in April 1972. These are of the first CLC cottage design and are believed to date from 1870. *Author*

Preston to Shrewsbury road (A49) where the summit of the line is reached after 1 mile 13 chains, having climbed about 75 feet from Winsford Junction.

The track is now on a level course and soon reaches another overbridge (No. 149) under a minor unmetalled road, Kennel Lane. Leaving the forest and entering an area of open heathland, there follows a straight, level stretch across Newchurch Common. On both sides of the line there are now attractive lagoons where there were formerly sand quarries. At 2 miles 17 chains there used to be Newchurch Crossing here with a minor road, and a crossing keeper's house on the up (north) side. Beyond, on the north side, new (early 1990s) housing has now been built on the site of Nova Scotia School. The descent down to the Weaver valley commences shortly before Whitegate station with an inclination of 1 in 133. The line entered the only intermediate station on the branch immediately after passing under bridge 151 carrying Clay Lane, which connects the small village of Whitegate, little more than a hamlet 1¼ miles to the north-east, with the much larger village of Little Budworth (population in 1981: 580) a mile further away to the south-west. The station contained a loop but had a platform on the up side only. The brick-built buildings were smaller than those on the main line but incorporated the usual house. Manley and Helsby stations had similar buildings. The timber signal box was at the Winsford end on the down side with the goods yard opposite. Here there were two long sidings but no goods shed or crane. Despite the loop, it would appear that no trains were ever scheduled to cross at Whitegate.

Soon after leaving the station the really steep descent to the Weaver begins, 1 in 80 and 1 in 82 for almost two miles all the way down to Falk's Junction, and known as Ellis's Bank. There was an Ellis's Farm on the north side and this is a pleasant area of dairy farming, typical of mid-Cheshire. The branch, now mostly on embankment, curves to the east past Marton Hole, the site of Marton Grange, and Marton Hall (all on the south side) and crosses over the Cuddington to Over road by bridge No. 153 at 3 miles 53 chains. Three-quarters of a mile further on was Ellis's level crossing (no house provided) and, at 4 miles 42 chains, bridge No. 154 over the Whitegate to Winsford road. Just beyond, the embankment ends and the line starts to veer away from the original authorised route by an angle of 8 degrees to the south, actually now heading due east.

When 4 miles 60 chains from Winsford Junction is reached the line has arrived at the limit of deviation allowed by Parliament from the original authorised route. From here on the railway was built without Parliamentary power; this had been applied for in the CLC Bill presented in 1867 and had been approved by the Lords' Committee but was subsequently withdrawn due to the failure of financial arrangements. All the land for the remainder of the branch was sold under private treaty by Lord Delamere who succeeded in adding a covenant whereby if the railway was built to Winsford it had to provide a public passenger and goods service for the benefit of the town, and not just for the use of the salt industry.

Three chains beyond this original limit was Catsclough Crossing, provided with a standard CLC crossing keeper's house, a ground frame in a small cabin and signals, even though it was a very minor road. The house still remains in occupation and others of the same design can also still be seen at Ollershaw

Whitegate signal box in 1912; the occasion is believed to be the inspection of the garden for the annual best-kept station competition. This box was opened on 10th August, 1891.

H. Gordon Tidey

The single-platform Whitegate station in May 1952, looking towards Winsford. The grounded body is one of the CLC's 4-wheeled third class coaches of 1874-1876.   *Gordon Biddle*

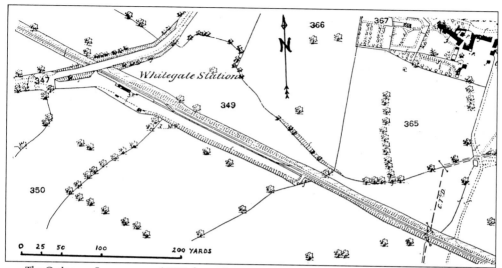

The Ordnance Survey map of 1877 shows the original layout at Whitegate. There was rail access to each end of the single goods siding. Note that only one signal post is shown, on the platform, which would have had an arm for each direction.

Reproduced from the 25", 1877 Ordnance Survey Map

Whitegate station.

Reproduced from the 25", 1910 Ordnance Survey Map

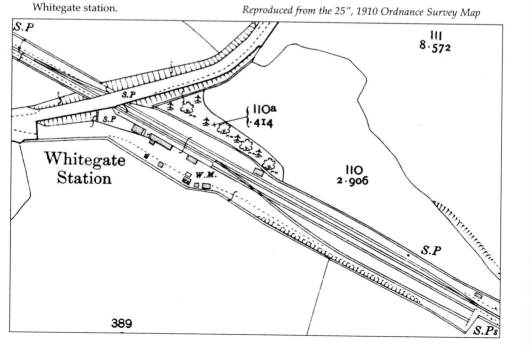

The crossing keeper's cottage at Catsclough in April 1990, a standard CLC design with the addition of a modern porch. There is track still in position even though the branch had closed in 1967.   *Author*

The original 1870 signal cabin at Falk's Junction (*on the right*), still just about standing immediately after the line closed in March 1967. It was of Manchester, Sheffield & Lincolnshire Railway design, and had become a lamp hut when replaced by a new signal box in 1891, which it was to outlive.   *Geoffrey Platt*

Lane Crossing on the Marston branch and a pair at Plemstall Crossing between Barrow and Mickle Trafford. It is likely that the other two crossing houses on the Winsford branch, at Wade's and at Newchurch Crossings, were also similar but both were demolished many years ago.

At Falk's Junction (5 miles 15 chains) there was a signal box and sidings and a branch was thrown off to the north-east, 26 chains in length, to H.E. Falk's Meadowbank Salt Works, entering the works at almost the same point as the termination of the authorised route, but approaching from quite a different angle. The gradient down to the crossing of the New Road (now Bradford Road) outside the works was not recorded but was quite steep, probably still at 1 in 80 or thereabouts. There was a single gate, opened by hand, across the line on the Cuddington side of the crossing which did not open across the road; instead trains were protected by the guard or fireman with a red flag.

From Falk's Junction the main route, which was doubled in 1892, turned to the south through a cutting and then followed the west bank of the Weaver for the remaining mile into Winsford and Over station, much of it cut into a shelf on the valley side. All along this section there were salt works continuously following the river bank on the down or east side of the line, with other salt works on the far side of the Weaver. The gradient down to Wade's Crossing (5 miles 38 chains), where there was a signalman's house and a signal box, was 1 in 113. Just beyond the crossing over Wade's Lane there was a trailing connection with Hickson's Salt Works' private siding. The down grade now eased to 1 in 261, but only for about 6 chains to the next trailing junction, this time with the line from the Knight's Grange (or Dairy) Salt Works.

Dropping down more steeply again, at 1 in 110, the sidings from Deakin's Over Salt Works trailed in at 5 miles 57 chains. After a further 13 chains the steep bank, which had dropped all the way from Whitegate, finally ended, and there was now a short rise for 9 chains at 1 in 110 up to Winsford signal box. On this latter section there was a bridge, No. 155, over a private drive, a level crossing of Baker's Lane which does not seem to have been protected in any way, and another trailing junction with the short branch from the Meadow Salt Works, which was reached by a swing bridge (not CLC property) over the River Weaver. From the signal box the line dropped more gently, at 1 in 310 and, throwing off a branch to the Dutch Salt Works with a facing connection, entered the terminus at 6 miles 8 chains from Winsford Junction (measured to the booking office?).

The original layout at the terminus included a single platform on the east side, a run-round loop, four sidings of which two ended at a wagon turntable, a goods shed, crane and loading bank, a small single-road engine shed, a water tower and a locomotive turntable. Adjacent to the station on the New Road was a terraced row of four railwaymen's cottages and next door was the Navigation Inn, which was on CLC land. Later the engine shed was widened to take two tracks, the disused turntable line extended to serve a foundry, the goods yard was enlarged with a new goods shed and the wagon turntable dispensed with, and two of the goods sidings were prolonged beyond the end of the yard and into neighbouring salt works. This allowed the official length of the Winsford and Over branch, to the CLC boundary gates at the far end of the goods yard, to be given as 6 miles, 12 chains and 19 yards.

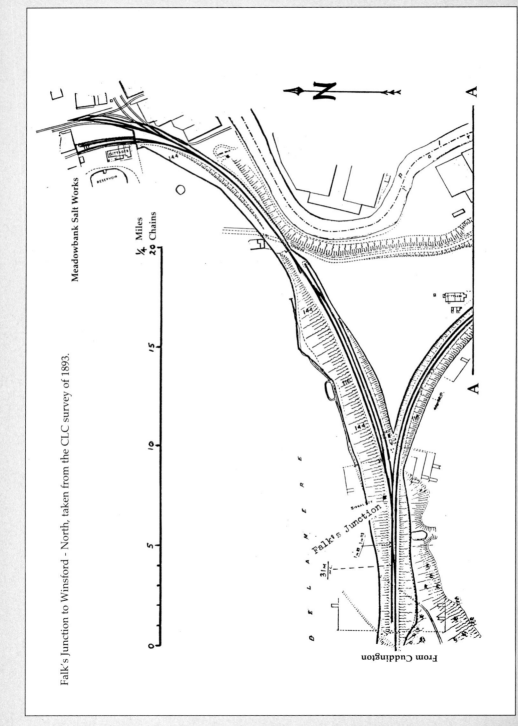

Falk's Junction to Winsford - North, taken from the CLC survey of 1893.

Meadowbank Salt Works

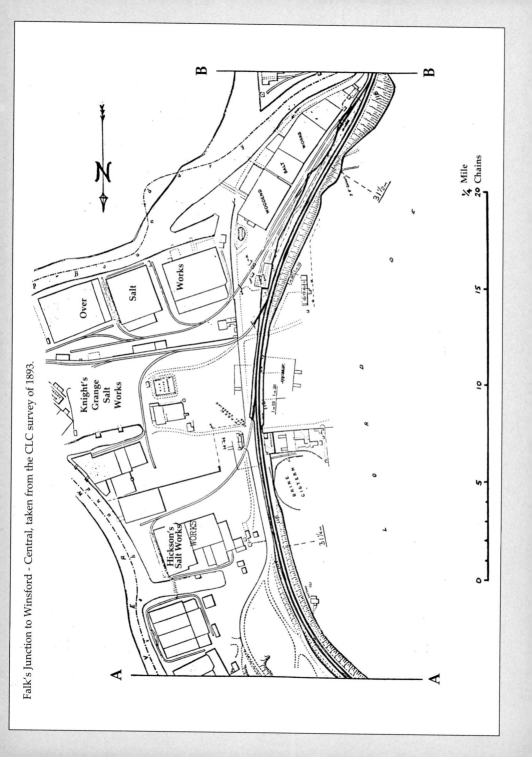

Falk's Junction to Winsford - Central, taken from the CLC survey of 1893.

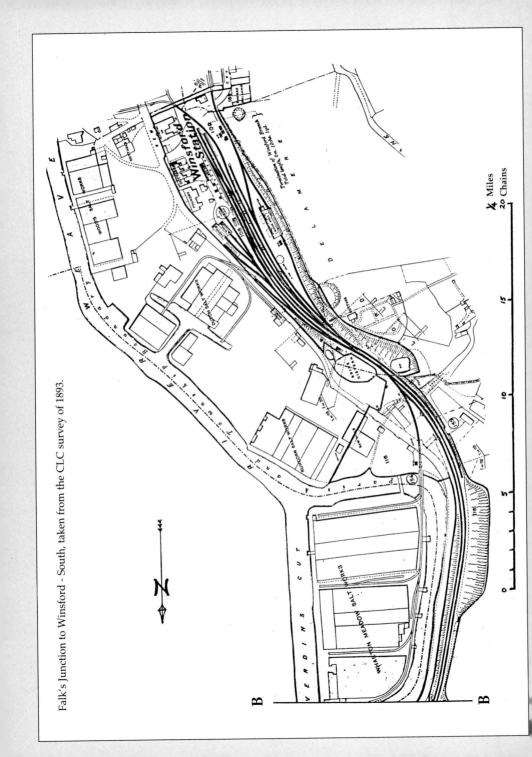

Falk's Junction to Winsford - South, taken from the CLC survey of 1893.

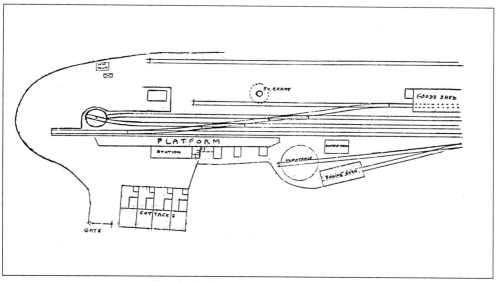

Winsford & Over station layout in 1872.

Winsford & Over station layout in 1927.

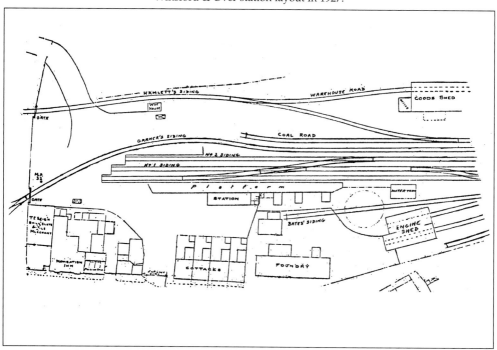

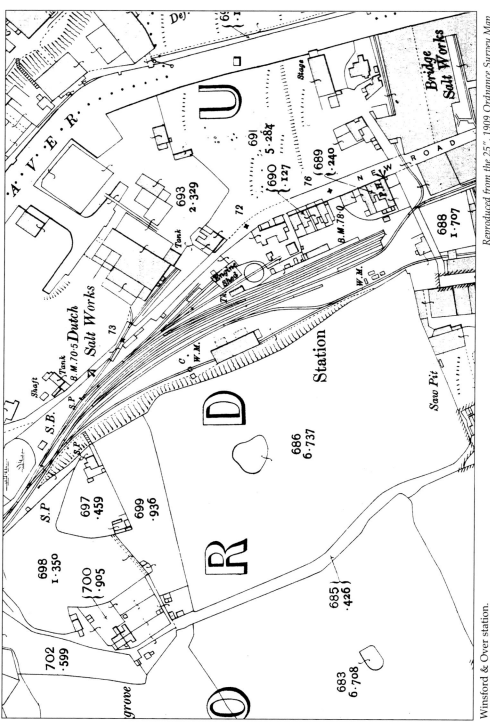

Winsford & Over station.

Reproduced from the 25", 1909 Ordnance Survey Map

Winsford and Over station in 1950, looking towards the terminal buffers, with Hamlett's Central Salt Works in the background. *James Boyd*

A close-up of the wooden station buildings, erected in 1870 as a temporary measure, at Winsford and Over in May 1952. The nameboard on the left is a concrete replacement. *Author*

The 1879 goods shed warehouse, with its handsome barge-boarding, easily eclipsed the meagre facilities provided for passengers at Winsford & Over station, as seen in this June 1952 view.   *Author*

The station buildings were a series of wooden huts, evidently intended to be temporary as there were plans to extend the line to join the North Staffordshire Railway at Sandbach. Powers for this extension were obtained through the Sandbach and Winsford Junction Railway Act on 27th June, 1872, but even though the MS&L was prepared to put in some money the scheme failed to attract sufficient capital and no work was ever started. It would have duplicated the LNWR's Sandbach to Northwich line, over which the North Staffordshire had obtained running powers. The temporary buildings remained to the end, and were never augmented.

Winsford and Over, looking from the terminal buffers back towards Cuddington in October 1953, on the occasion of a visiting railtour.   *G. Dudley Whitworth*

Chapter Three

Building the Line

No attempt had been made by the West Cheshire Railway to start construction of any of its line before being taken over by the CLC, so the first action of the new owners was to invite tenders from suitable contractors. John Sheldon Wilkinson was engaged as Resident Engineer for the new works under Charles Sacré, the CLC's Chief Engineer. Wilkinson's monthly reports to the Committee give a clear idea of the progress being made (or lack of it) once construction had actually got under way. Enough ground for a double track line was purchased, but only a single line was built on the branch to Winsford.

Tenders from various firms of public works contractors for building the West Cheshire Railway, including the Winnington branch and the first 4 miles 60 chains of the Winsford branch, were opened on 8th February, 1866 and included the following:

	£	s.	d.
Benton & Woodiwiss	189,742	9	1
G. Wythes	194,758	8	6
Logan & Hemingway	196,958	1	6
Eckersley & Bayliss	199,118	1	4
Brassey & Company	233,300	0	0
Waring Brothers	252,000	0	0

That from Benton & Woodiwiss, whose home base was at Glossop, was the one accepted. George Benton had been a railway contractor since 1854, and had taken Abraham Woodiwiss into partnership in 1861. The firm seems to have continued in business until at least 1886. The contract was signed on 1st May, 1866 and a copy of the Indenture can be inspected in the Public Record Office at Kew under reference RAIL 110/121.

The construction of the West Cheshire main line started in March 1866 (before the contract was signed), but it was not until early in 1867, January or February, that work on the Winsford branch commenced. On 20th February the Engineer reported that a start had been made with the earthworks and fencing, and on 15th May he reported that the works on the branch were now in full operation. A further contract worth £8,995 was awarded to Benton & Woodiwiss on 21st August, 1867 for stations on the West Cheshire line. This modest amount clearly could not cover all the stations involved and is believed to be only for the three smallest, namely Manley, Helsby and Whitegate, which were all alike. The Engineer's estimate for the cost of the other stations, in addition to this small contract, amounted to £39,638, and it is thought that this sum was in respect of Northwich, Hartford, Cuddington, Delamere and Mouldsworth. Note that Winsford station is not included in these figures.

On 22nd April, 1868 Wilkinson was able to report that the permanent way was now laid over the first four miles of the branch, and the next 60 chains of track were evidently completed by 17th June when it was reported that work

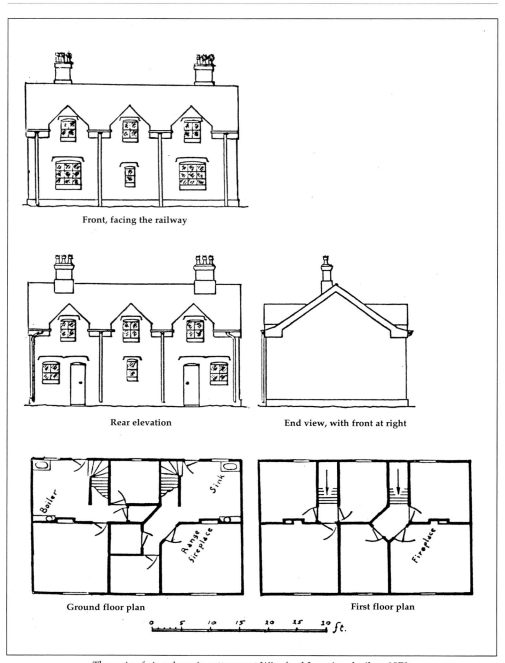

Front, facing the railway

Rear elevation

End view, with front at right

Ground floor plan

First floor plan

The pair of signalmen's cottages at Winsford Junction, built *c.* 1870.

was now stopped at 4 miles 6 furlongs pending a decision on the extension. This was waiting for an agreement with Herman E. Falk to be finalised about access to his salt works and the requisite land purchase from Lord Delamere, as previously explained.

At last tenders for the construction of the extension of the branch into Winsford including the terminal station were invited, and amongst those opened on 21st October, 1868 were:

	£	s.	d.
Benton & Woodiwiss	14,462	18	1
Barnes & Beckett	16,850	0	0
Logan & Hemingway	17,578	17	6
Brassey & Company	18,163	15	4

Again that from Benton & Woodiwiss was the one accepted. The contract was not to be executed until arrangements had been made to acquire the land, and this was still the position on 18th February, 1869. However, on 17th March it was reported that work had finally started on the extension, even though all the land had still to be purchased. The Engineer stated, on 21st April, that the extension was in a forward state so far as land purchases permit, and on 14th July he reported that the earthwork of the extension was in an advanced state except for Winsford and Over station which was held up by non-possession of land. However, the last parcel of land was evidently obtained from Lord Delamere soon afterwards, but only after the insertion of the restrictive covenant that was to cause the CLC so much trouble and expense in later years. The total cost of the branch inclusive of land, stations and cottages was said to be £150,000.

On 30th and 31st July, 1869 Lt Col Hutchinson for the Board of Trade made his first visit to the completed portions of the line, and on 20th October Wilkinson, the Resident Engineer, reported that earthwork on the extension was now virtually complete. The following month the Board of Trade officer made a second inspection, and on 18th May, 1870 it was announced that goods traffic would commence on the branch from 1st June, although the Winsford station was not quite ready for passengers. This had to await a further inspection on 26th May by Colonel Hutchinson. Extracts from his report are quoted in an Appendix.

Only the identity of one of Benton and Woodiwiss's locomotives to work on the West Cheshire contract is known for certain. This was an inside-cylindered 0-6-0 saddle tank built by Manning, Wardle & Co. of Leeds (No. 239) in 1867 for Benton & Woodiwiss and delivered new to them at Northwich. This engine later belonged to Read Brothers of Sowerby Bridge with the name *Samson*. During 1870 Benton & Woodiwiss took delivery of engines numbered 12, 13, 14, 16 and 17 which suggests they owned at least 10 other locomotives at this period. Not a lot is known about their earliest locomotives but there were three which were used on contracts completed in 1865-66. It is not known where they were next used and thus they might have come to the West Cheshire. However, it should be pointed out that Benton & Woodiwiss were also engaged in several contracts for the Midland Railway (Duffield-Wirksworth, Derby-Melbourne-

Breedon, Sawley-Weston and Trent Bridge, Nottingham) and one for the Furness (branch to Newby Bridge) during 1867-70, so there is only a slight chance (one in six) that any of these three engines came to the West Cheshire.

One was an 0-6-0 tender engine built by Kitsons of Leeds about 1855 for James Taylor of Accrington, who named her *Whitmore*. Taylor had a permanent way contract with the MS&L until he failed in 1860, leaving the MS&L as his largest creditor. They acquired Taylor's plant including this locomotive which became MS&L No. 132 in July 1861, and resold the engine (by now nameless) in September 1864 to Benton & Woodiwiss, who used her on their Marple to New Mills contract of 1864-65. Another engine on the same contract was an 0-6-0 side tank with inside cylinders built by Dodds of Rotherham in 1865. What happened subsequently to these two engines is not known. The third possible contender for working on the West Cheshire construction was another Manning, Wardle (No. 181) 0-6-0ST named *Woodiwiss* and built in 1865 for Benton & Woodiwiss for use on their Wakefield-Stainforth contract, completed in 1866. This engine later belonged to the contractor Walter Byrom with the name changed to *Bradford*. It is a pity that there is not more information available about the contractor's locomotives used in building the line.

Charles R. Sacré, Engineer of the Cheshire Lines Committee 1866 to 1874, and Carriage & Wagon Superintendant 1866 to 1886.   *Author's Collection*

Edward Ross, Secretary of the West Cheshire Railway until 1865, and Secretary of the Cheshire Lines Committee from 1863 until 1892.   *Author's Collection*

Chapter Four

Early Days

The main line of the West Cheshire Railway opened to goods traffic between Northwich and Helsby on 1st September, 1869, followed by the Winsford branch on 1st June, 1870. Passenger services, by mixed train only, were introduced between Northwich and Helsby from 22nd June, 1870 and it had been planned to do the same on the branch, but Winsford and Over station was still not quite ready. Nevertheless just nine days later, on 1st July, a passenger carriage was attached to two goods trains each way on weekdays between Cuddington and Winsford, soon increased to three per day. Needless to say, the slow service by goods train did not attract many passengers, and the service was withdrawn from 1st January, 1874 after less than 3½ years. The CLC owned its own passenger coaches and goods wagons but not any locomotives. These were hired, complete with driver, fireman, and all fuel and lubricants required, from the Manchester, Sheffield & Lincolnshire Railway.

There was much local agitation for the service to be restored; public meetings were held and a petition was drawn up. The CLC's attitude can best be presented by quoting the following letter sent by the CLC to J.H. Cooke Esq. of Winsford, which was reproduced on 21st September, 1878 in the *Warrington and Mid Cheshire Examiner*:

September 17th, 1878

Dear Sir

I am favoured with your letter of the 13th September with reference to a petition from the ratepayers of Winsford and neighbourhood asking that passenger trains might be run on our Winsford branch. This petition was presented to the Cheshire Lines Committee at their meeting in June last when they decided that they could not comply with the prayer of the memorial. When a passenger service was formerly run, the result was a loss to the Committee; and the line being a single one, the running of passenger trains materially interfered with the the working of the coal and salt traffic for which traffic the line was made

Yours faithfully,

Edward Ross (Secretary)

Mr Ross seems to have conveniently forgotten that no separate passenger trains had run over the branch. Meanwhile, the goods traffic was increasing without the incumbrance of any interfering passengers. In 1873 it was decided to build a branch into the salt works of Joseph Verdin & Sons which was on an island in the river and thus would require a swing bridge to be built over the original river course on the western side of the works; the east side was a man-made cut of the Weaver Navigation known as Verdin's Cut and built in the 1790s. At one time, before the cut was made, there had been a lock on the river here called the Butty Meadow Lock. This is the reason the salt works here was named the Meadow Works.

The plan of this new line was deposited with the Clerk of the Peace for Cheshire at 3.00 pm on 29th November, 1873 and it is interesting as it shows the complete layout of Winsford and Over station as it existed at that time. It can be inspected in the Cheshire Record Office, Chester Castle under their reference QDP 519 (the reference for the 1861 Deposited Plan is QDP 388). The line was to commence 10 chains to the north of Winsford booking office and was one furlong, two chains and 70 links in length. (There are 10 chains in a furlong and 80 chains in a mile, and 100 links in a chain.) It was necessary to obtain an Act of Parliament in order to bridge the Weaver and this received the Royal Assent on 30th July, 1874 (Vict. 37/8, cap. 169). Traffic over the completed new branch commenced in October 1876. The CLC latterly owned only the first five chains of the branch. Maintenance of the swing bridge was transferred to the Salt Union by agreement of October 1926.

Also in the mid to late 1870s siding connections were put in for the Knight's Grange Salt Works and for Hickson's Salt Works, whilst the original 1870 siding to the Deakin's Over Salt Works was completely altered and enlarged; the exact dates for these alterations have not been identified but they had been completed by 1881.

In 1878 it was proposed to put in a connection to the Central Salt Works of George Hamlett and Sons by extending one of the sidings at Winsford station across the south end of the goods yard, whilst an additional siding was required in the yard for salt wagons. It was decided to use the space occupied by the goods shed for the additional siding, and widen the goods yard to provide a new goods shed immediately west of the existing building. Most of this work was carried out during 1879, the tender of Aaron Haughton for the new depôt for £1,410 being accepted on 16th September, 1878. Soon after another siding was extended the same way through the southern end of the goods yard to serve the Bridge Salt Works of J. Garner & Co. However an undated plan suggests that the new goods shed and the connections to Hamlett's and Garner's were completed before the additional siding was laid. This latter was certainly in position by 1893.

Goods traffic by February 1886 was such that four trains each way were now required daily. The Winsford Local Board had taken up the case for the re-introduction of passenger services pointing out that Lord Delamere's covenant required the CLC to provide such a service. The Committee reluctantly agreed and as the block system of signalling was being introduced between Northwich and Mouldsworth (completed in July 1886) it was decided to extend it also to the Winsford branch as far as Whitegate. This was ready for inspection on 6th July, 1886 but the Board of Trade officer, when he inspected 18 days later, was critical of the sidings points at Whitegate still worked by capstan and noted only a six-lever frame at the Winsford end of the platform (without mentioning if it was housed in a cabin or was open). It is presumed that the block telegraph instruments were in the booking office at this time. Nevertheless, he sanctioned the reopening of the branch to passengers.

Notwithstanding the inspection date, the branch had been carrying passengers since 1st May, coaches being attached to three of the four daily goods trains. The time taken for a single journey to or from Cuddington varied between 25 and 50 minutes. As before, there was no Sunday service. Possibly from May 1886, and certainly by August 1888, it had been necessary to introduce a fifth (evening) goods working. A good idea of the running arrangements at this period may be gleaned from the reports of the only major accident to a train in the life of the Winsford branch, which occurred on Saturday 25th August, 1888, fortunately without loss of life. The weekly *Warrington Advertiser* for Saturday 1st September had this to say in the rather prosaic prose of the period:

Railway Accident at Winsford

An accident of an alarming nature happened to the 12.15 train from Winsford and Over Station, Cheshire Lines Railway, on Saturday morning. The train which consisted of several empty trucks, two passenger carriages, brake van and engine left the station and proceeded about a quarter of a mile when by some mistake or other it ran into a siding of Messrs Deakin Limited, salt proprietors, where there were several trucks of coal, one of them being smashed to atoms, the buffers of the engine meeting the same. One of the carriages was smashed as was also the brake van, the brakesman being severely injured. He was carried to his lodgings and thence conveyed to his home at Northwich. Several of the passengers were shaken but no serious injury is reported.

Another report quotes the engine and carriages being thrown off the rails and that three passengers were severely shaken. The guard, John Tench of Northwich, sustained serious internal injury. The breakdown gang cleared the line in the course of the afternoon. It is interesting to note that the guard should lodge in Winsford even though he only lived in Northwich. Was this for domestic reasons or was it because his duty started at Winsford at 6.00 am?

At the inquiry the guard gave his name as Charles Tench (not John) and said he received injuries to his back and shoulder. One of the six passengers was reported to have injured a thumb. The engine, 0-6-0 No. 130, had arrived at Winsford on the 10.50 am mixed train from Cuddington some 20 minutes early (due 11.40), evidently running tender first. After five minutes it set off light engine to collect seven empty coal wagons from the Knight's Grange Siding. The shunter was busy unloading fish, with the help of the consignee, at the station platform, and the station master had disappeared into his office, so the lad numbertaker (age 17) went on the engine to help the guard attend to the points and couplings. The lad, Joseph Lightfoot, said this was the first time he had done this; the guard said he had helped on every occasion during the five weeks and three days he had been goods guard on the Winsford branch. The lad said the guard asked him to help; both the guard and the shunter said he went of his own accord.

After collecting the coal empties the train stopped just short of the points for Deakin's Siding, the guard uncoupled the engine and it ran forward clear of the points which were then changed by the lad to allow the engine to reverse into the siding. The wagons were then allowed to run by gravity down the grade until they had passed over the points whereupon the guard applied a wagon brake to bring them to a stand in about 12 wagon lengths. The engine then left the siding and the guard coupled it to the wagons. No one thought to check if the lad had reset the points for the main line; he hadn't. The engine, with everyone back on board, then propelled the wagons back to the station where

A Sacré class '23' 0-6-0 No. 25 in 1886. In February of that year sister locomotive No. 50, built
one month later in 1861, was working as the Winsford branch engine. The sandwich frames are
a feature of the older members of this class.   *Real Photographs 1024*

Sacré class '24' 2-4-0 No. 183, then stationed at Northwich, waits to back onto the coaches of a
Chester line train at Manchester Central in 1887. This locomotive was to take her turn as one of
the Winsford branch passenger engines from 1892 until about 1903. The single spectacle
McKenzie & Holland signals were replaced in 1892.   *Author's Collection*

they were attached to the front of the train in the platform. This consisted of a first and second class composite coach, a third class brake, and a goods brake van in the rear.

The driver, John Berry, had been with the MS&L for 27 years, 16 as driver and the last 14 years working from Winsford. He said the train was travelling at 18 to 20 mph up the 1 in 106 [sic] gradient when he noticed the points were wrongly set about 60 yards ahead. He immediately applied the steam brake and got his fireman, who was firing at that moment, to screw on the tender hand brake, then he whistled for the guard's brake. The guard did not hear the whistle and did not apply his brake; he was riding in the goods brake van. The 18 coal wagons in Deakin's Siding were 103 yards clear of the points but that was not a sufficient distance in which to halt the train, which was doing about 5 mph when the collision occurred.

One of the standing wagons was badly broken and one derailed. The engine broke a life guard and the vacuum pipe and was derailed. The goods brake van and the composite coach were damaged and the brake third carriage was also derailed. Note that the vacuum brake was not connected to the train; the coaches were unlikely to have been fitted anyway.

The station master, George Stocks, had been in railway service for 30 years of which the last 18 had been with the CLC; he had been station master at Winsford since the beginning of 1880. The CLC held him to be responsible for the accident by neglecting to see that the shunter, Jesse Wallis, performed his proper duties. The unfortunate Stocks was demoted or, as one newspaper put it, 'is to be reduced in consequence of the recent disastrous accident'. The inspecting officer Col F.H. Rich picked out Stocks for blame but also included the contributions of the driver, guard and shunter in his condemnations. However his report was highly critical of the CLC in allowing passenger trains to work over a line not properly signalled and with no interlocking with the points. All the points on the main line were worked by capstans and most (including Deakin's Siding) were only protected by disc signals actuated by the points; i.e. point indicators. He also complained that many of the sidings and connections had never been approved by the Board of Trade. His report is dated 8th September but it was not until 25th September, 1888 that a copy was sent to the CLC.

A month later this was followed up by a letter from the Board of Trade requiring the CLC to complete the interlocking on the branch without delay. The Committee estimated that this would cost £7,500, which could not be justified, so on 10th November they gave notice that passenger services would cease as from 1st December, 1888. Only a few months previously representations had been made to the CLC requesting them to increase their train service on the branch from the present three each way per day.

Again the Winsford Local Board agitated for the service to be restored and again the CLC refused, so the Local Board instructed their solicitors to apply to the Court of the Railway and Canal Commission for an Order, requiring the CLC to provide reasonable facilities for the carriage of passengers over the branch, on the grounds that Lord Delamere's covenant was not being adhered to. The case was heard at the Royal Courts of Justice in London some two years later on 25th February, 1891 when the court agreed with the Local Board and granted the Order.

Having lost the case, the CLC now set about the task of bringing the branch up to standard without delay. New signal boxes and improved signalling were provided at Whitegate, Falk's Junction, Wade's Crossing and Winsford (Winsford Junction had to wait until 1896 for a new box). As all the salt sidings between Falk's Junction and Winsford faced towards Winsford it was decided to double the track between these points so that all the connections trailed into the down line. Further, this down line was to be used by down goods trains only; all passenger as well as up goods trains were to use the up line. Thus there were no facing points against passenger trains whilst the CLC was saved the expense of interlocking the points on the down goods line. It was also agreed to run separate passenger-only services; no more mixed trains. This would require two locomotives to be based at Winsford, one passenger and one goods, so the little engine shed was widened from one to two tracks. Col Hutchinson made his inspection on 25th January, 1892 and reported the work well executed, except some facing point locks required adjustment and the heights of main line signals should be made greater than those of goods and loop lines. Provided these were put right in a fortnight he sanctioned the re-opening of the branch to passengers, which was inaugurated seven days later on 1st February.

A wagon label for a consignment from Winsford. Wagon No. 913 was an 8 ton covered goods van built by the Ashbury Railway Carriage & Iron Co. Ltd in 1874.

Chapter Five

Working the Line

At the opening of the branch in 1870 the line was operated under Train Staff and Ticket regulations, with the red and white staff or tickets kept in the booking offices at Cuddington and Winsford stations. From 1886, probably on 1st May and certainly by 24th July, block working in addition was introduced between Cuddington and Winsford Junction, and from there to Whitegate. It is believed the block telegraph instrument was in the booking office at Whitegate. Trains were not crossed at Whitegate, just the single staff remaining for the branch. Then on 1st February, 1892 the Absolute Block system was applied to the whole branch, with the instruments in the signal boxes, in addition to the staff and ticket working. The line was now divided into two sections, each with its own staff or tickets. One was Cuddington (not Winsford Junction) to Falk's Junction (blue) and one for Falk's Junction to Winsford (red staff and tickets). On the new down goods line station yard working was introduced, with a special code of bell signals. By March 1907 it had changed to Permissive Block working, still with the special bell codes. The up line was worked by single line block as it was used by down passenger trains.

Trains on the branch could only pass each other at Falk's Junction. A branch train could not pass another branch train on the double line between Winsford Junction and Cuddington but it could pass a Chester line train. Under the staff and ticket system a ticket was issued to a driver if a following train was due before a train returning through the section in the opposite direction. If no following train was scheduled, the staff was issued.

The branch had its own telegraph circuit, known as circuit 'T', and Cuddington with the call signal 'CD' was the controlling point. The other telegraph instruments on the circuit with their call signals were:

Winsford Junction box	WJ	Wade's Crossing box	WB
Whitegate box	WG	Winsford box	W
Falk's Junction box	FJ	Winsford & Over Station	WK

Cuddington had to check each point every morning except Sundays and report the state of the circuit to Northwich. In addition, if any defect was found it had to be immediately reported to the telegraph inspector at Warrington Works, where the CLC had its Signal and Telegraph works.

All signal cabins had to display two boards outside, one diamond shape (for signals) and the other an oval (for the telegraph). One side was painted white and was exposed if the signals and instruments were in good order but the red side was displayed if any defect had been found. The use of these fault boards was still practised in 1907 but had generally ceased by 1914. However the January 1918 Supplement to the Timetable Appendix quotes the boards as still having to be exhibited at six locations on the CLC, one of which was Catsclough Crossing. Repairs were the responsibility of the district lineman at Hartford for signals, point rodding, locking gear, etc., or at Mouldsworth for the telegraph wires and instruments.

GREAT NORTHERN,
MANCHESTER, SHEFFIELD, AND LINCOLNSHIRE, AND MIDLAND
JOINT RAILWAYS.

Circular No.

REGULATIONS FOR WORKING TRAFFIC
OVER THE SINGLE LINE BETWEEN WINSFORD AND CUDDINGTON.

Train Staff and Ticket.   1. A Red and White Train Staff, or Train Ticket, must be carried with each Train to and fro, without which no Engine or Train must be allowed to leave Winsford for Cuddington, or Cuddington for Winsford.

Two or more Trains.   2. If another Engine or Train is intended to follow before the Staff can be returned, a Train Ticket, stating Staff following, must be given to the person in charge of the leading Train, and the Staff itself must be given to the person in charge of the last Train; after which no other Engine or Train must be allowed to follow, *under any circumstances whatever*, until the return of the Staff.

Train Tickets where kept.   3. The Train Tickets are to be kept in a box fastened by an inside spring; the key to open the box is the Train Staff, so that a Ticket cannot be obtained without the Train Staff.

Ticket Boxes.   4. The Ticket Boxes are to be fixed in the Booking Offices at the Winsford and Cuddington Stations.

Authorised person to receive and deliver the Staff or Ticket.   5. The Clerk in charge, Inspector, or the person in charge for the time, is the sole person authorized to receive and deliver the Train Staff or Train Ticket.

Taking Staff and Ticket too far or not at all.   6. A Guard or Engineman taking a Staff or Ticket beyond the Station to which it belongs, or leaving a Station without the Staff or Ticket, as heretofore explained, will subject himself to dismissal, although no accident may arise.

Guard to show Engineman Staff or Ticket.   7. Enginemen must not start from Winsford for Cuddington, or from Cuddington for Winsford, until the Train Guard has shown them the Train Staff or Train Ticket.

Usual "Engine following" signal to be used.   8. The usual Special Train signal, "Engine following," must be used for the guidance of Plate-layers, &c.

Coal and Ballast trains.   9. Coal and Ballast Trains are to be treated in every respect like Passenger Trains, as regards the Staff and Ticket arrangements.

Engine or train breaking down.   10. In the event of an Engine or Train breaking down between two Telegraph Stations, the Fireman must take the Train Staff to the Telegraph Station in the direction whence assistance is expected, that the Train Staff may be at that Station on the arrival of the Pilot Engine. Should the Engine or Train that fails be in possession of a Train Ticket instead of the Staff, *assistance can only come from the Station at which the Train Staff has been left*. The Fireman is to accompany the assistant Engine to the place where he left his own Engine.

WM. ENGLISH, Manager.

19, James-street, Liverpool,

The original single line regulations for the branch issued in 1870.

For the opening of the branch in 1870 only two signal boxes were provided, at Winsford Junction and at Falk's Junction; both believed to have been placed in the vee of the junction. That at Falk's was a timber box of early MS&L design and it is likely that Winsford Junction box was the same, especially as the one at Mouldsworth was also of this type. The ground frame at Catsclough Crossing had a cabin which looked like an early MS&L type and may have dated from the opening of the line. It is not known if any of the other ground frames on the branch were provided with cabins.

Cuddington had to wait until 1886 before it was provided with a signal box, possibly from 1st May; it was ready for inspection on 6th June. An all-timber box of the first CLC standard design, it contained a 30-lever frame. It was abolished on 15th November, 1970. At the Northwich end of the goods yard was a ground frame cabin with 16 levers which also probably dated from 1886 (certainly by 1893). This was replaced by an open 2-lever ground frame on 25th November, 1956 and lasted until about March 1964.

The new signal box and loop at Whitegate opened at noon on Monday 10th August, 1891. The all-timber box contained 24 levers of which 5 were spare and it, like all the other new boxes on the branch, was to the second CLC design which showed some detail differences compared with the first type at Cuddington, but was generally quite similar. It had ceased to be a block box from 1st February, 1892, and closed on 6th July, 1947. On that last day it reopened as a block post for a few hours whilst the three replacement ground frames were installed. The last of these open frames closed on 19th July, 1964, the others a little earlier.

At Falk's Junction the new box, on the north (down) side of the line, had 20 levers including 6 spare and was brought into use at noon on Tuesday 29th September, 1891. The old box was ordered to be removed, but it remained in its place and was used as a lamp room. The new signal box became a staff station (block post) on 1st February, 1892, and ceased to be a block post from 1st January, 1931. It is believed to have been abolished about the same time as Whitegate (July 1947) and duly demolished leaving the old box still there but out of use; it was standing (just about) looking very dilapidated when the line finally closed in June 1967.

There was also a new box, together with new gates and new signals, at Wade's Crossing, brought into use at noon on Tuesday 22nd September, 1891. The frame contained 8 levers, all in use, but did not control the siding connections to Hickson's or to the Knight's Grange Works. Although closed as a block post in 1931 this box seems to have lasted longer than the others (because of the crossing) and may have remained in use until the line beyond Falk's Junction closed on 1st May, 1965.

Winsford station had to manage without a signal box until one was opened at 6.00 am on Monday 11th January, 1892 on the down side opposite the entrance to the goods yard. It had a 30-lever frame, including 4 spare levers. It ceased to be a block box from 1st January, 1931 but its closure date has not been established; it may have been sometime before October 1953, possibly in July 1947 along with Whitegate and Falk's Junction cabins.

Whilst all this new signalling work was being carried out on the branch in 1891, the original 1870 box at Winsford Junction had to soldier on for a few more years. It is believed that a new locking frame was fitted in 1886 containing 13

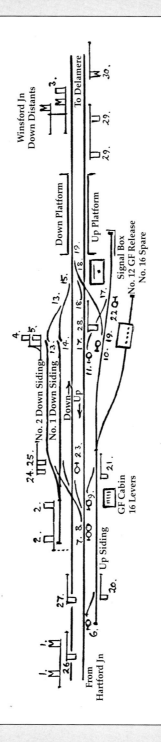

Signalling diagram of Cuddington station *c.* 1910.

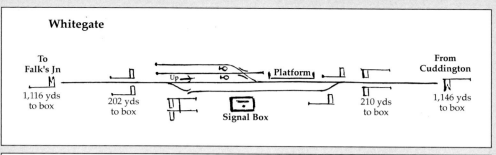

Whitegate

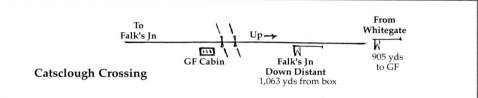

Catsclough Crossing

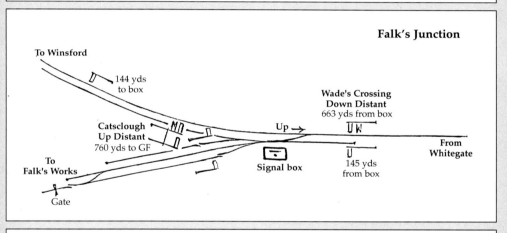

Falk's Junction

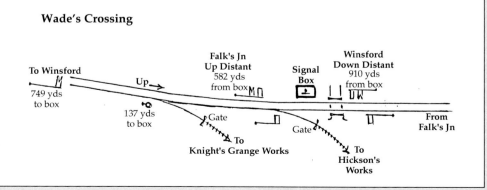

Wade's Crossing

The new signalling on the branch in 1891. The Inspecting Officer was critical of the arms of the goods line signals being at the same height as those to be used for passenger trains. They were subsequently altered.

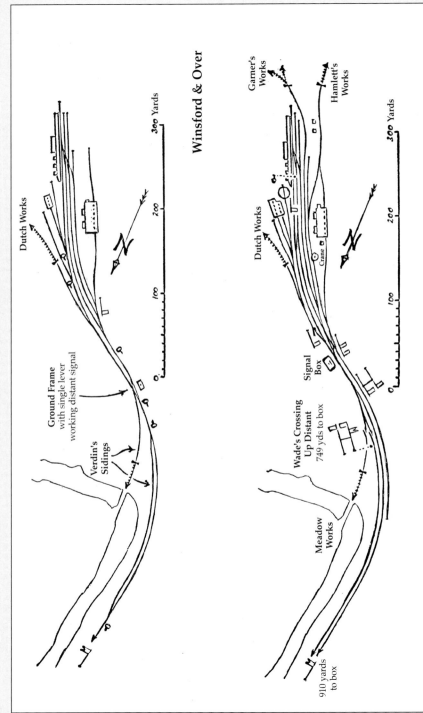

Track layouts and signals at Winsford & Over in 1881 (*top*) and in 1892 (*bottom*).

working levers and 3 spare and it became a block post at the same time. In February 1889 an additional safety switch was ordered to be fitted three yards inside the branch up home signal, and there were more signal alterations during the week ending 31st October, 1891. Finally a replacement box came into use at 12.30 pm on Sunday 29th October, 1896 and this brought up to date all the signalling between Cuddington and Winsford. The new all-timber box, on the north (up) side of the line, was of the second CLC standard design, and was finally abolished on Sunday 11th February, 1968 even though all the track had not been recovered from the branch.

Turning attention to the ground frames (or dwarf frames as the CLC sometimes called them) it is not known for certain if there was one originally at Newchurch Crossing but, if there was, it had gone by 1893. At Ellis's Crossing the frame and signals were ordered to be taken away as from 22nd September, 1891 and the gates altered so as not to open across the line. At Catsclough, from noon on Tuesday 13th October, 1891, the distant signals were re-sited, the home signals removed and lamps were put on the gates. In effect, the gates acted as signals. The frame had four levers; two for the distants, one for the gate locks and the other spare. There were other ground frames on the line at Whitegate, Wade's Crossing and Winsford until they were all replaced by signal boxes in 1891-92 as described.

An instruction of 1918 stated that fogsignalmen were not to be stationed at the up and down distants for both Whitegate and Wade's Crossing, and at the down distant for Falk's Junction. These signals may have been permanently fixed at caution by this time as was common on single lines, and it rather suggests that fogmen were provided for some of the other distant signals on the branch when necessary; namely the up distants for Winsford Junction and Falk's Junction, and the down distant for Winsford and Over station. In addition, the Catsclough Crossing distant signals may also have been similarly protected during fog.

As to the signals themselves, Cuddington and Whitegate at first will have been provided with double-armed (one for each direction) three-position signals with double, red and green, spectacles. The third position of the arm was straight down inside a slot in the post. Junction and distant signals, and the station signals after the introduction of block working in 1886, were of two positions only, with a single red spectacle; the clear position being indicated by a white light which did not need a spectacle glass. In 1893-94 a green light was substituted for white which meant a return to double spectacles. This was due to the possible confusion with other white lights following the introduction of gas lighting in towns. At the same time the small back lights on the signal lamps, which had hitherto been green, now changed to white. Shunting arms and ground signals generally had a purple light instead of red, and also used purple for the back lights. Oil lamps were used for the signal lights.

The characteristic vee notch at the end of distant arms was introduced about 1873, although it was probably another two or three years before the branch signals were altered. A straight white stripe was painted on the front of the red arms until 1910 when a white chevron was adopted. The next change took place from January 1926 when an amber light replaced red for caution, and the fronts of the arms were now painted yellow with a black chevron. However, it was late 1928 before the distant signals in the Cuddington - Winsford area were altered.

The signal cabin at Winsford Junction, which was commissioned on 29th October, 1896 and abolished on 11th February, 1968. It was only a little longer (13 ft 1 in.) than it was wide (12 ft 4 in.); porter-signalman F. Saunders is standing on the landing in this view *c.* 1946.   *Trevor Booth*

Following the final cessation of passenger services from 1st January, 1931 the line was operated under the One Engine in Steam regulations, with a single key staff for the whole branch housed in Winsford Junction signal box. The trailing siding connection to the down goods line from the Knight's Grange Works was taken out (the siding was still listed in 1929 although the works had closed much earlier) and in its place a new facing connection was put in for the Over Works. This enabled the up line to be severed just past this junction, and it was lifted from here until just before the trailing connection with the Meadow Works siding. One reason for this was subsidence, to be detailed shortly. From now on the two ends of the former up line were worked as two sidings, one from Falk's Junction and the other from Winsford station. All through goods trains in both directions now used the former down line.

The subsidence mentioned was caused by saturating the salt beds under the ground with water, and pumping out the resultant mixture, known as brine. The subsidence caused endless trouble to the railway, and affected nearly all the track from just east of Whitegate station. It was thought that the opening of the branch might have to be postponed when a huge hole, 140 yards in diameter, suddenly appeared only 300 yards south of the railway at Marton. This is now an attractive lake known as Marton Hole. At various times a warning was issued that Ellis's Bank (from Whitegate right down to Catsclough) was continually sinking and drivers approaching in either direction must keep a sharp look-out and be prepared to stop their trains if necessary. Such warnings are known to have been issued in February 1892 and for several weeks following, December 1894, August 1895, May 1904 and March 1907. Doubtless there were other occasions which have not been brought to notice.

On the double-track section between Hickson's Siding and Meadow Works Siding the line was built on a shelf cut into the valley side, the down line being on embankment and the up line in cutting. It was the down line that at times was severely affected by the subsidence. One particularly bad slip occurred in December 1917 when just short of the last half-mile into Winsford had to be closed, cutting off the Knight's Grange, the Over, the Wood End and the Meadow Salt Works. A temporary buffer stop was installed about 100 yards south of Hickson's Siding. If there was traffic after dark the engineer's watchman had to place a red light on the buffer stop. No train or engine was permitted on the down goods line at the Winsford station end. Fortunately the weekly notice issued on 25th January, 1918 made no mention of this and presumably normal services over the down line had by then resumed. Previously, in February 1916 subsidence had caused the connection to the Wood End Salt Works to be closed, and the up line had to be slewed.

The tickets issued to passengers in the initial 1870 to 1873 period were printed by the MS&L for the CLC and were distinguishable in having negative numerals at the ticket ends, that is the actual figures used the colour of the card and only the black background was printed. By the time the line reopened to passengers in May 1886 the CLC had established its own ticket printing section as part of the Stores Department in Warrington Works, and the tickets now had positive numerals printed in black without any special background. Another difference was that the new tickets had the fare printed on the front. The standard colours

The up starting signal at Cuddington, a typical CLC lower quadrant design introduced in 1893, photographed in August 1970 after the track in the goods yard had been lifted; the down sidings still remain.   *Author*

for the card were white for first class, pink for second class and green for third class. On return tickets the standard colours were used for the return half on the left, with a different colour for the outward half on the right: yellow, blue and buff for first, second and third classes respectively. Sometimes the two halves exchanged colours on tickets with reduced fares. Children's issues had a semi-circular cut away portion along the bottom edge for easy identification.

Second class had been abolished on the Cheshire Lines when passenger services recommenced in 1892. By 1913 the use of separate colours for the outward half of return tickets had been discontinued; instead a large letter 'R' was overprinted on the return half in black. Pink, the former second class colour, was now commonly used for cheaper issues such as day returns and excursions, along with buff, although other colours were also used. Dog tickets were buff or cream, bicycle tickets were also cream whilst those for prams were orange. On 1st January, 1917 there was a 50 per cent fare increase and to distinguish new printings from old stocks of tickets the new fare was depicted as *Actual fare*. From 6th August, 1920 there was a further 25 per cent increase and new tickets were now printed with the words *Revised fare* on the face. From 1st January, 1923 there was a slight reduction and just the word *Fare* was quoted, as on pre-1917 tickets.

After the Winsford branch had finally closed to passengers, the separate CLC Stores Department was taken over jointly by the LMS and LNER as from 1st April, 1933. New tickets were printed for the CLC by these two companies, who both allocated numbers to every station, and these numbers (known as audit codes) were printed on the tickets. Curiously, the LMS allocated the numbers 5052 and 5053 to Whitegate and to Winsford and Over even though these stations were closed. It is thought that this was in case any special excursions were arranged. Certainly one football excursion from Winsford to Chester is known to have run in 1931 after closure, and there may well have been others.

One important but seldom mentioned function performed on the railways was the daily collection of the cash takings and returns from every station on the line. Lockable cash boxes were provided for this purpose and strict regulations governing how they should travel were stipulated. In 1907 the cash boxes from Winsford and Whitegate were handed to the guard of the 8.15 am train (8.05 in 1918) each morning, then given into the care of the clerk in charge at Cuddington station who handed them, with his own cash box, to the guard of the 8.33 am train (8.27 in 1918) from Chester for conveyance to Manchester Central. The empty boxes returned daily on the 11.45 am train from Central, and then forward on the 4.10 pm (3.02 in 1918) from Cuddington.

The gas-lit coaches in use on the branch until *circa* 1926 needed to be topped up with gas regularly and for this purpose the CLC gas reservoir wagon No. 3310, built at Gorton in 1899, was stationed at Winsford. It was a four-wheel wagon 30 ft 9 in. long over buffers with a large cylindrical tank and was fully fitted to work in passenger trains. In December 1917 it was rostered to be attached to the rear of the 4.10 pm train from Winsford every Monday and Thursday. At Cuddington it was detached and waited for the 6.05 pm milk train from Chester for dispatch to Cornbrook for filling. A special stop at 8.14 pm was made on those days to detach the tank wagon at Cornbrook, where the CLC had its oil-gas works. The filled vehicle was returned to Winsford every

Tuesday and Friday by attaching to the 10.45 am empty milk train from Manchester Central to Chester, again a special stop being made at Cornbrook. Arrival at Cuddington was at 1.30 pm and the gas tank was next attached to the rear of the 3.02 Workmen's train (previously the 5.35 pm ordinary train) to Winsford. With the arrival of electrically-lit stock at Winsford about 1926 the tank wagon was transferred away (it was at Tiviot Dale for a time) and eventually fell into disuse early in the 1939 war.

The Cheshire Lines owned its own passenger carriages and goods wagons but all the locomotives it required were hired from the MS&L and its successors the Great Central Railway (GCR) (as from 1st August, 1897) and the LNER (as from 1st January, 1923). They were hired complete with driver, fireman and all coal and lubricants needed, and were paid for on a mileage rate except that shunting and pilot work was charged by the hour. There were also hourly payments for engines held on stand-by and there was a fixed charge for locomotives specially steamed but not required. The hire accounts were made up quarterly and the rates varied at different periods.

In 1901 the charges were 10d. per mile for passenger engines, including light engine miles; 12½d. per mile for goods engines; 5s. 5d. per hour pilot work, shunting, banking and on stand-by; and a fixed charge of £2 18s. 0d. for an engine specially steamed. For just one quarter in 1901 Winsford was debited with 301 hours 15 minutes for pilot and shunting duties. Separate figures for the branch trains were not given, but presuming only the scheduled services were run - seven passengers per day Monday to Friday and six on Saturday, four goods per day Monday to Saturday - for all the 13 week period, and 12 miles were charged for each return branch working, then the quarterly passenger and goods mileages would have amounted to 6,396 and 3,744 respectively. This would have resulted in a total quarterly charge for all locomotive and crew hirings for the Winsford branch of £543 1s. 0d., the equivalent of an annual payment of just over £2,172. This does not include the mileage between Winsford Junction and Cuddington, which would have added a further £308 or so.

Winsford engine shed was a sub-shed of Northwich, and was CLC property, being leased in turn to the MS&L, GCR and LNER. The engines at Winsford were exchanged from time to time with others of the same class among Northwich's allocation. Until 1915 all branch trains worked only as far as Cuddington and, as there was no turntable there, it became pointless to use Winsford's turntable and it soon fell into disuse; it was not included in a list of CLC turntables dated 1907. Nevertheless, it was not until 1912 that any tank engines were stationed at Winsford, so there was considerable tender-first running.

Train guards were CLC employees, as were all other railwaymen except enginemen. When the branch first opened in 1870 both passenger and goods guards were paid 24 shillings per week, whilst signalmen earned 22 shillings after two years' service and porters 20 shillings, also after two years. They all received a free dark green uniform.

The responsibility for operating the Winsford branch rested with the Cheshire District traffic inspector, whose office was at Northwich. From 1884 to 1900 he was S. Denning, who later became station master at Liverpool Central. In the early 1900s the inspector was B. Roberts, whilst in the 1920s he was Ernest Garner.

Chapter Six

Locomotives and Train Services

There is unfortunately no information about Winsford's locomotives in the earliest days until one moves on to Friday 12th February, 1886. All four goods trains that day were worked by MS&L engine No. 50, a double-framed Sacré 0-6-0 of class '23'. The enginemen signed on duty at 6.00 am and set off from Winsford with the first goods train at 7.00 am. During the day they managed to have two hours' rest and arrived back with the last goods at 6.30 and signed off at 7.30 pm, a total of 13½ hours. The journey to Cuddington was rated at seven miles, so all four return trips amounted to 56 miles. In addition another six miles were added for each of the six hours spent shunting, so No. 50 was credited with having run a total of 92 miles that day. Then on Saturday 25th August, 1888 it was the turn of No. 130, of the same class, to work the three mixed and one goods train scheduled for that day. At this time the enginemen's hours were given as 5.30 am to 8.30 pm, and that of the goods guard as 6.00 am to 9.00 pm.

Including Nos. 50 and 130, there was a total of 10 of these class '23' 0-6-0s stationed at Northwich Shed at this period, the one outstationed at Winsford sub-shed being changed from time to time. It is quite possible that these engines, which were built between 1859 and 1867, had operated the branch trains since its inception, and they probably continued to do so until about 1902 when the later Sacré inside-framed 0-6-0s of class '18' took over. These mixed trains of 1870-73 and 1886-88 seemed only to have included two of the four-wheeled carriages in their makeup; a first and second class composite and a brake third.

When the separate passenger service began on 1st February, 1892 it was first and third class only as second class had been abolished on the CLC from the beginning of the year. The trains probably consisted of a four-coach set of four-wheel coaches, all built before 1877, and they are likely to have lasted on the branch until six-wheel stock took over around 1905. The passenger engine will have been one of three Sacré double-framed 2-4-0s of class '24' built in 1865-67 and then allocated to Northwich - Nos. 57, 183 and 264. By the turn of the century they seem to have been replaced by the similar but later class '12A' 2-4-0s, including Nos. 164 and 169, both built in 1885.

The passenger service from 1892 was exactly double that which had previously been given to Winsfordians as Mixed trains. Departures from Winsford were at 8.10 and 9.25 am, 12.25, 4.10, 5.50 and 7.20 pm, the journey taking 20 minutes except that the 4.55 pm ex-Cuddington was allowed an extra five minutes. The last train got back to Winsford at 8.35 pm. The service provided up to 1902 was very similar, but from 1903 an additional train left Winsford at 5.20 pm and Cuddington at 6.00 pm on Mondays to Fridays only, on which days the 5.50 pm was retimed to leave the terminus at 6.25.

Two photographs of the branch passenger train at Winsford taken between 1906 and 1911 show class '12A' No. 169 ready to set off for Cuddington tender first. The four carriages in the train, all six-wheeled, are made up of a birdcage brake third

49

CHESHIRE LINES.

RE-OPENING

OF THE

WINSFORD & OVER BRANCH

FOR

PASSENGER TRAFFIC.

The Branch Line from CUDDINGTON to WINSFORD and OVER will be RE-OPENED for Passenger traffic on MONDAY, February 1st, 1892, and the following service of PASSENGER TRAINS will commence running on that date.

STATIONS.		WEEK DAYS.					
		A.M.	A.M.	P.M.	P.M.	P.M.	P.M.
WINSFORD AND OVER ...... dep		8 10	9 25	12 25	4 10	5 35	7 20
WHITEGATE .... ,,		8 20	9 35	12 35	4 20	5 45	7 30
CUDDINGTON .... arr.		8 30	9 45	12 45	4 30	5 55	7 40

	dep.	A.M.	A.M.		P.M.	P.M.	P.M.	P.M.	P.M.	P.M.	P.M.	P.M.
		8 36	8 45	9 51	12 54	12 54	4 43	4 47	6 4	6 33	7 49	8 13
CHESTER (Northgate) ...... arr.		9 5	—	—	1 30	—	5 13	—	6 35	—	8 22	—
HAWARDEN .... ,,		9 44	—	—	1 59	—	5 44	—	7 14	—	9 24	—
WREXHAM .... ,,		10 18	—	—	2 30	—	6 18	—	7 48	—	—	—
NORTHWICH .... ,,		—	8 55	10 2	—	1 5	—	4 58	—	6 43	—	8 23
KNUTSFORD .... ,,		—	9 15	10 17	—	1 26	—	5 15	—	7 3	—	8 41
MANCHESTER .... ,,		—	9 50	10 45	—	2 10	—	6 3	—	7 48	—	9 23

STATIONS.		WEEK DAYS.										
		A.M.	A.M.	A.M.	A.M.	A.M.	P.M.	P.M.	P.M.	P.M.	P.M.	P.M.
MANCHESTER .... dep.		7 28	—	9 33	11 40	—	3 38	—	—	5 7	6 37	—
KNUTSFORD .... ,,		8 7	—	10 12	P.M. 12 23	—	4 13	—	—	5 35	7 16	—
NORTHWICH .... ,,		8 24	—	10 32	12 41	—	4 32	—	—	5 52	7 37	—
WREXHAM .... ,,		—	8 5	—	—	11 10	—	—	—	—	—	6 30
HAWARDEN .... ,,		—	8 37	—	—	11 42	—	3 41	—	—	—	7 2
CHESTER (Northgate) ...... ,,		—	9 20	—	—	P.M. 12 25	—	4 16	—	—	—	7 40
CUDDINGTON .... arr.		8 35	9 50	10 13	12 52	12 53	4 42	4 46	—	5 37	7 48	8 11

	dep.	A.M.		P.M.		P.M.		P.M.		P.M.	
CUDDINGTON .... dep.		8 40	10 50	1 0		4 55		6 10		8 15	
WHITEGATE .... arr.		8 50	11 0	1 10		5 5		6 20		8 25	
WINSFORD AND OVER ...... ,,		9 0	11 10	1 20		5 20		6 30		8 35	

S.—Saturdays only.

All Trains are First and Third Class.

Liverpool Central Station, January, 1892.

DAVID MELDRUM, Manager.

J. H. WILLIAMS & CO., Printers, 8, School Lane, Liverpool.

No. 17

WEDNESDAY, JANUARY 11th, 1899

No. 13.—SPECIAL HUNTING TRAIN.

A SPECIAL HUNTING TRAIN will leave Manchester (Central) at 9 0 a.m. for WINSFORD.

Mr. KIRK to provide Engine, Carriages, Horse Boxes, and Guard, and arrange for the Train to stop at intermediate Stations as required.

Tickets on the outward journey to be collected at Cuddington.

A sharp look-out must be kept for the return of this Special between 4 0 p.m. and 5 0 p.m. Mr. KIRK to be advised by wire the time return Special leaves.

Particulars of the Bookings by the above Train must be wired to me immediately after the departure of the Train.

☞ The Line must be kept Clear, and Clerks-in-Charge at Roadside Stations must acquaint all Persons concerned at their respective Stations and make all necessary arrangements. Guards are requested to make out Reports immediately on the arrival of the Special Trains, and send them in without delay.

The Receipt of this Notice must be acknowledged by NEXT TRAIN.

Liverpool Central Station,
Jan. 5th, 1899.

DAVID MELDRUM, Manager.

WORKING TIMETABLE FOR OCTOBER 1902

Weekdays only

UP TRAINS

UP TRAINS	Goods	Pass	Pass	Empty coal	Goods	Pass	Goods	Pass	Pass	Exp. goods SX	Pass
	a.m.	a.m.	a.m.	a.m.	a.m.	p.m.	p.m.	p.m.	p.m.	p.m.	p.m.
Winsford	6.30	8.10	9.25	9.45	11.10	12.20	3.30	4.10	5.50	7.35	7.50
Whitegate	-	8.20	9.35	T	-	12.30	T	4.20	6.00	A	8.00
Cuddington { arr.	-	-	-	-	11.45	-	-	-	-	8.00	-
Cuddington { dep.	7.00	8.30	9.45	-	12.00	12.40	4.10	4.30	6.10	8.10	8.10
Northwich { arr.	-	-	-	10.15	12.10	-	-	-	-	8.20	-
Northwich { dep.	-	-	-	11.15	-	-	-	-	-	8.35	-
Haydock Colliery	-	-	-	1.35	-	-	-	-	-	10.00	-
Heaton Mersey Sdgs.	-	-	-	-	-	-	-	-	-	11.20	-

DOWN TRAINS

DOWN TRAINS	Exp. goods MX	Goods Z	Goods H	Pass	Pass	Pass	Goods Y	Goods SX	Pass SO	Goods	Pass SX	Goods	Pass	Pass
	a.m.	a.m.	a.m.	a.m.	a.m.	p.m.	p.m.	p.m.	p.m.	p.m.	p.m.	p.m.	p.m.	p.m.
Heaton Mersey Sdgs.	1.30	-	-	-	-	-	-	-	-	-	-	-	-	-
Haydock Colliery	-	-	-	-	-	-	-	-	-	-	-	3.15	-	-
Northwich { arr.	2.30	-	7.55	-	-	-	1.15	4.00	-	-	-	6.30	-	-
Northwich { dep.	-	-	8.10	-	-	-	1.30	4.15	-	-	-	-	-	-
Cuddington { arr.	-	-	-	-	-	-	-	-	-	-	-	-	-	-
Cuddington { dep.	-	7.30	8.32	8.45	10.45	1.10	1.40	4.30	4.55	5.00	5.20	-	7.00	8.25
Whitegate	-	D	D	8.55	10.55	1.20	-	D	5.05	-	5.30	-	7.10	8.35
Winsford & Over	-	8.05	9.00	9.05	11.05	1.30	3.20	4.55	5.15	5.25	5.40	-	7.20	8.45

Notes: A = Stops to ATTACH when required.   D = Stops to DETACH when required.
H = To work HAYDOCK train.   T = Stops for TRAFFIC purposes when required.
Y = Performs shunting at Falk's Siding.   Z = Does shunting at Falk's Siding.

of 1879 with three compartments leading, followed by a five-compartment third class coach, a four-compartment coach which was probably a composite but could be an all-first, and at the rear (Winsford) end of the train another brake third but this time with normal roof without the birdcage lookout for the guard. The last three coaches were all built before 1888. If a composite was included there would be seating for 130 third class and 16 first class passengers

There was probably a subtle change of livery which the sharp-eyed may have noticed with the arrival of these six-wheelers on the branch. Traditionally all CLC carriages had varnished teak bodies with white roofs and bronzed green underframes. Starting in 1901 many coaches that were more than about 20 years old were no longer re-varnished when they were repaired; instead they were painted in what the CLC called 'oak brown'. This was applied complete with imitation graining and feathering and, at first glance when new, was almost indistinguishable from the genuine varnished teak. The bronzed green eventually gave way to black paint from about 1915, and became a brown shade similar to teak in colour after 1923. A transfer of the Cheshire Lines armorial badge was applied only to carriages with first class compartments.

The body of one of the old four-wheeled third class coaches was placed alongside the platform at Whitegate for use as a storage hut, and it was still there as late as 1953 painted brown below the waist and a stone colour on the top half. Another similar coach body was at Cuddington station; indeed these old coach bodies were quite a feature at many CLC country stations.

A photograph taken at Cuddington about the same period (1906-11) as the Winsford pictures shows what is believed to be the branch goods train with a class '18' 0-6-0 working chimney first towards Winsford and with an old goods brake van of 1869-74 vintage at the back. Three headlamps are carried on the buffer beam which is thought to be a special branch headcode. The contemporary photograph of No. 169 on the branch passenger train shows no headlamps at all, but possibly the engine had only just run around its train. The number of the 0-6-0 is not very distinct but could be 29XB, the 'X' indicating an unreadable digit. Numbers 290 to 299 were all class '18' built in 1872 and all except 295 and 297 received the 'B' suffix to denote duplicate stock in 1907. The last one of this batch was withdrawn in 1913.

There were several of these class '18' 0-6-0s at Northwich until about 1909-11, when they were replaced by the Parker 0-6-0s of classes '9B' and '9E' (LNER class 'J9') built between 1891 and 1894. Eventually, in February 1921, there were no less than 27 of these engines stationed at Northwich, and one or other in turn would have been sub-shedded at Winsford. The 1890s had seen the goods traffic on the branch reach its peak. With the reintroduction of passenger trains, and the additional shunting now required at the salt works, the branch goods engine only had time to fit in three return trips during each day. So Northwich had to make at first one, then two, additional return workings on the branch, making five goods trains in all although the fifth did not run on Saturdays.

In 1902 the timetable showed the Winsford engine leaving the terminus with trains at 6.30 am, 11.10 am through to Northwich, and 3.30 pm; with returns at 7.30 am from Cuddington, 1.15 pm from Northwich, and 5.00 pm from Cuddington. The return of the first working was marked in the timetable as

No. 169 and her train at Winsford some time between 1906 and 1911. The absence of any headlamps on the tender suggests that the locomotive has only just run round her train.

Author's Collection

The platform at Winsford and Over on probably the same occasion as the previous photograph, with the branch train of four 6-wheeled coaches waiting to leave for Cuddington. The engine is a Sacré class '12A' 2-4-0 No. 169; note the absence of passengers and the wooden nameboard.

J.A. Peden C2717

'Does shunting at Falk's Siding' whereas the second return trip quoted 'Performs shunting at Falk's Siding'. This subtle difference in wording would appear to denote when this shunting took place. The first train was only allowed 35 minutes for the entire journey including a stop at Whitegate, and clearly had plenty of time from 8.05 am to go off and do the shunting at Falk's Works before getting back to Winsford for the 11.10 am departure. In contrast the second train was allowed 100 minutes for the journey from Cuddington without a Whitegate stop, so clearly performed the shunting *en route* as arrival back at Winsford at 3.20 pm was only 10 minutes before it had to set off again.

The two Northwich workings on the branch in 1902 were interesting. The first got to Winsford at 9.00 am and then took the 9.45 departure for Haydock, on the GCR St Helens line, reversing at Skelton Junction and arriving at Haydock Colliery with its train of empty coal wagons at 1.35 pm with stops at Cuddington, Northwich and Knutsford. It left the colliery at 3.15, presumably with all the wagons loaded with coal, again reversed at Skelton and calling only at Knutsford to take water arrived at Northwich at 6.30 pm. The other goods train ran on Mondays to Fridays only, leaving Northwich at 4.00 pm and taking 55 minutes to Winsford. It then became the 7.35 pm (SX) to Heaton Mersey Sidings (Stockport), arriving at 11.20 with stops at Whitegate, Cuddington, Northwich, Lostock Gralem, Hale and Skelton - despite which it was described in the timetable as an 'Express goods'! The return early on Tuesday to Saturday mornings set off at 1.30 am and ran non-stop to Northwich in exactly one hour.

The goods timetable for Winter 1917-18 shows three weekday trains from Winsford to Cuddington and return, the last one extended to Northwich if required. There was also an evening goods on Mondays to Fridays which started at Northwich at 7.20 pm for Winsford and did not get back until 12.15 am the following morning. This was clearly worked by a Northwich engine, with the other three being entrusted to the Winsford goods engine. All four trains were booked to cross passenger trains once on each return trip at Falk's Junction. Changes were introduced for the May 1918 timetable; the first morning departure from Winsford, which previously was at 6.00, was now shown as light engine only at 6.15 am to Cuddington, whilst the Northwich evening working ran much earlier, returning to Northwich at 9.30 pm (SX) and passing passenger trains at Falk's on the return as well as outward journeys.

Returning to the passenger services, the Winter 1909-10 timetable included two extra trains on Mondays only and one extra on Wednesdays. The Saturday service had also been increased, to seven each way as for the rest of the week. The 1914-15 Winter service showed a reduction by one train on each day except Saturdays. The following Summer timetable was the same except that the lunchtime working from Winsford at 12.20 was extended on Fridays only through to Northwich, arriving at 12.48 pm. This is the first time any of the branch passenger trains had ventured any further than Cuddington.

About 1916, in the middle of the war, additional Workmen's trains were introduced into the branch workings, two of them operating on Sundays - the first time any trains had run on the branch on a Sunday. The main reason seems to have been the establishment of armament factories at Lostock Gralem and Plumbley West, a new platform being provided at the latter place, and the 4.50

WORKING TIMETABLE FOR JANUARY 1918

Weekdays (Mondays to Saturdays)

UP TRAINS

UP TRAINS	Work mens a.m.	Work mens a.m.	Goods a.m.	Pass a.m.	Pass a.m.	Goods a.m.	Pass p.m.	Work mens p.m.	Goods p.m.	Pass p.m.	Goods p.m.	Pass p.m.	Work mens p.m.	Pass p.m.	Pass p.m.	Work mens Goods p.m.	Goods SX p.m.
Winsford	4.50	5.20	6.00	8.05	9.22	11.35	12.20	12.50	3.35	4.10	–	–	4.50	6.10	7.35	8.50	11.10
Whitegate	5.00	5.30	R	8.14	9.32	R	12.29	1.00	R	4.20	–	–	5.00	6.18	7.45	9.00	A
Cuddington	5.09	5.39	6.30	8.22	9.42	12.01	12.37	1.09	4.10	4.30	–	–	5.09	6.27	7.35	9.09	12.00
Northwich	5.20	5.50	–	–	–	–	N	1.20	R	–	–	–	5.30	–	–	9.20	12.15
Knutsford	5.39	6.19	–	–	–	–	–	–	–	–	–	–	–	–	–	–	–

DOWN TRAINS

DOWN TRAINS	Work mens a.m.	Work mens a.m.	Goods a.m.	Pass a.m.	Pass a.m.	Pass SX p.m.	Work mens SO p.m.	Goods p.m.	Work mens SX p.m.	Goods SO p.m.	Pass p.m.	Goods SO p.m.	Pass SX p.m.	Work mens p.m.	Pass p.m.	Pass p.m.	Work mens p.m.	Goods SX p.m.
Knutsford	6.10	–	–	–	–	–	2.50	–	–	–	–	–	–	6.30	–	–	–	10.40
Northwich	6.30	6.55	–	–	–	Y	2.50	–	5.35	5.55	5.30	6.00	5.48	6.30	–	–	8.40	B
Cuddington	6.40	7.07	7.40	8.45	11.30	1.15	3.02	5.10	5.38	D	5.15	D	5.58	6.42	7.05	8.05	8.10	10.52
Whitegate	6.50	7.17	R	8.55	11.40	1.25	3.11	D	5.48	5.25	5.25	6.00	–	6.52	7.15	8.15	9.00	11.02
Falk's Jc (a.)	–	–	8.05	–	–	–	2.00	5.35	–	–	–	5.55	–	–	–	–	8.40	–
Falk's Jc (d.)	–	–	8.25	–	–	–	2.50	6.00	–	–	–	6.00	–	–	–	–	9.00	–
Winsford	7.00	7.27	8.35	9.05	11.50	1.35	3.00	3.20	5.58	6.10	–	6.10	–	7.02	7.25	8.25	9.10	11.12

Sundays:

Up

	Work mens a.m.	Work mens p.m.
Winsford	6.50	4.50
Whitegate	7.00	5.00
Cuddington	7.09	5.09
Northwich	7.20	5.20
Knutsford	–	–

Down

	Work mens a.m.	Work mens p.m.
Knutsford	8.40	6.40
Northwich	8.51	6.51
Cuddington	9.00	7.00
Whitegate	–	–
Falk's Jc	–	–
Winsford	9.10	7.10

Notes:

A = Calls to ATTACH only.

B = Departs Northwich 7.20p.m. SX to convey full wagon loads only to Falk's Junction or Winsford.

D = Calls to DETACH only.

N = Arrives NORTHWICH 12.48p.m. on Fridays only, also ECS on Saturdays only.

R = Calls when REQUIRED.

Z = Departs KnutsFord ECS at 6.40a.m.

Y = Departs Northwich 12.55p.m. on Fridays only.

A 1908 view of the Winsford branch goods (*right*), with a class '18' 0-6-0 standing alongside on the up line at Cuddington.   *A.G. Turves*

The Winsford branch goods stands on the down line before entering Cuddington station *c.* 1908. The engine is a Sacré class '18' 0-6-0. Note the headlamp code.   *A.G. Turves*

A Parker Great Central class '3' 2-4-2T No. 583, here seen in Manchester, which was one of the Winsford branch locomotives in 1921-22 and probably for some of the preceding years. The 6-wheeled third brake carriage is of the same design as those used on the branch at this period.

Author's Collection

A Parker 0-6-0 as LNER No. 661c of class 'J9', about 1924. This engine, along with several others of the class, was stationed at Northwich at this period, and took turns to work the Winsford branch goods trains.

Real Photographs W390

and 5.20 am departures from Winsford ran through to Knutsford. The other three weekday Workmen's, and the two on Sundays, all worked through to Northwich, and the last train on weekdays did not get back to Winsford until 11.12 pm. Immediately it arrived the late evening goods to Northwich set off. These trains were in addition to the ordinary branch service of six trains each way daily (not Sundays) whilst the lunchtime working was now extended to Northwich on Saturdays as well as Fridays. The branch thus had no less than 11 passenger and 4 goods trains scheduled daily each way.

Not only were there more trains, they were longer as well. Two train sets were required, both stabled and cleaned at Winsford. One set consisted of nine carriages - two brake thirds and seven all-thirds - all six-wheeled, gas lit, and not steam heated, having seats for 410 passengers. The other set comprised seven carriages - two brake thirds, four all-thirds and one composite - again all six-wheeled and not steam heated, having seats for 260 third class and 12 first class passengers. This set worked the 5.20 am Workmen's and all the ordinary passenger trains, hence the composite. A special set was made up for the Sunday service - two third brakes, five all-thirds and the composite - eight coaches in all. Why the composite was included is not known. Were there first class workmen (workgentlemen?) to be conveyed? If so it was most unusual, possibly unique. These Workmen's trains did not appear in the public timetable and ordinary passengers were not supposed to use them. Incidentally, the platform at Winsford and Over station was very short, only long enough for six of the coaches, and that at Whitegate was also very short.

The Sacré 2-4-0 passenger engines had departed by 1912 and the building of new tank locomotives for the Marylebone suburban service enabled one of the older Parker 2-4-2T locomotives of class '3' (LNER class 'F1') to come to Winsford, the allocation being increased to two for the additional wartime trains. In February 1921 Northwich Shed was home to Nos. 583, 600 and 726, built 1890-92, and any two of these in turn would have been sub-shedded at Winsford. This was the first time tank engines had been used on the branch; also two tank engines would fit on one road in the little engine shed leaving the other track free for the Winsford goods tender locomotive. No. 583 had her round-top firebox replaced by one of the Belpaire type in March 1915; the other two already had Belpaire fireboxes when they first came to Winsford.

A month after the war had ended the timetable for December 1918 showed a reduction to three weekday Workmen's trains but still the two Sunday trips were retained. These now all terminated at Northwich, the through workings to Knutsford having been discontinued. These Workmen's trains seem to have carried on for a few more months but it is not known exactly when they, and the Sunday service, finished. The timetables for 1921 and 1922 were made up of a basic service of seven trains each way, with an extra train on Wednesdays and Saturdays. Several of the trains now ran through to Northwich. Only one set of coaches and one passenger engine were now required.

The latter was a Parker 4-4-0 tender engine of class '2A' (LNER class 'D7'), the tank engines having been sent away. At Grouping on 1st January, 1923 there were six of this class at Northwich, Nos. 701 to 704, 707 and 709 of which one in turn would be the Winsford engine. In 1926 an additional member of this class, LNER No. 5708, came to Northwich. It was about 1926 that bogie coaches at last

An LNER (ex-Great Central) class 'D7' 4-4-0 No. 5703, which was transferred to Northwich in 1922, and is believed to have been the Winsford branch locomotive during 1924.

Author's Collection

A Pollitt 0-6-0 as LNER No. 5146 (formerly 5809) of class 'J10' at Northwich in 1947. This engine, along with several others of the same class stationed at Northwich, took turns to work the Winsford branch goods trains at this period.   *Author*

replaced the ancient six-wheelers on the branch. The train was now rostered for two bogie coaches, a lavatory composite and a third brake. They were steam heated and electrically lit and the provision of lavatory accommodation for what was now only a 17 minute journey was luxury indeed. There would be seating for 89 third class and 17 first class passengers.

The Summer 1928 and the following Winter timetable showed a reduction from seven to six basic weekday trains but there were still eight on Saturdays. The extra Wednesday trains had now gone and the only through working to Northwich was one of the Saturdays-only trains. The goods timetable currently included two weekday trains, 6.45 and 11.15 am, from Winsford to Cuddington, the second one crossing a passenger train at Falk's Junction (or more likely while shunting at the Meadowbank Salt Works, but this is not shown in the working book). There was also a Saturdays-only goods from Winsford at 3.25 pm which ran through to Northwich, getting back at 7.20 pm. In addition there was the Mondays to Fridays working from Northwich which ran somewhat earlier than it did in 1919. This was now the responsibility of the Northwich No. 3 Yard Shunting Engine which spent the morning working the Baron's Quay branch and shunting at Northwich. Then at 1.00 pm it set off with brake van only for Lostock Gralem in order to take the 2.25 pm (SX) goods from Lostock to Winsford. The return journey was to Northwich only, reached at 6.27 pm.

From the end of 1924 the LNER class 'J10' 0-6-0s started to appear on the Northwich (and Winsford?) goods trains, becoming more and more frequent although the 'J9s' continued to play some part until 1936. On 29th October, 1928 two class 'F1' 2-4-2T locomotives returned to Northwich in the shape of Nos. 5587 and 5589. From now until July 1929 these two engines took turns to be the regular Winsford passenger engine and the 4-4-0 tender locomotives were seen no more.

In 1929 the CLC purchased four steam railcars, or steam coaches as they were called, and the first of them, No. 600 which was added to stock on 2nd July, made a special trial run from Stockport to Winsford on 8th July, arriving at noon. Evidently the trial proved successful as another of the steam coaches, No. 602, was sent brand new to Northwich on 16th July, 1929 expressly to take over the branch passenger workings.

The steam coach was partially built by the Sentinel Waggon Works Ltd at Shrewsbury (their No. 7743) and sent to Nottingham where the coachwork was added by the Metropolitan-Cammell Carriage, Wagon & Finance Co. More usually being quoted as being built by Sentinel-Cammell, it was one of the six cylinder 100 hp type similar to the later LNER cars, and cost £3,750, having seating for 59 third class passengers but no first class. Most seats had throw-over backs so that passengers could choose which direction to face. Once the crew had been trained to operate the car it took over the entire service and so the Winsford branch became third class only later in July 1929.

No. 602 was stationed at Northwich and thus had to work as empty stock to Winsford before the first morning train, and similarly back to Northwich after the last train. The driver and fireman were hired from the LNER but if a guard was required he would be a Cheshire Lines man; however it seems the car operated without a guard, the fireman covering his duties. These steam coaches were included in the CLC's coaching stock and were not treated as locomotives.

The only known photograph of the CLC's Sentinel-Cammell steam coach No. 602 working the Winsford branch in 1929-1930, here seen at Whitegate. It looks as if the driver and all the station staff are waiting for the photographer to get back on the coach.   *Author's Collection*

This interior view of a Sentinel-Cammell steam coach is actually of one of the LNER vehicles, but No. 602 was very similar. Note the throw-over seat backs, and the hanging straps for standing passengers.   *Author's Collection*

Steam coach No. 602 in later years, on a Liverpool to Stockport working passing Skelton Junction in 1939.
Geoffrey Platt

A close-up of steam coach No. 602 seen at Liverpool Brunswick shortly before it ceased working in August 1944.
Real Photographs W8072

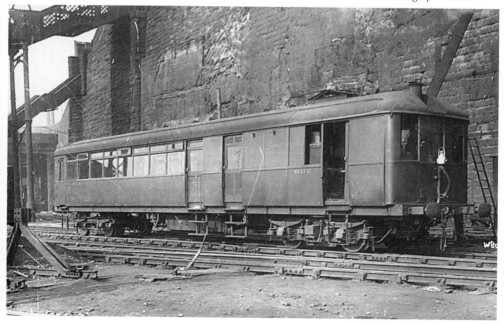

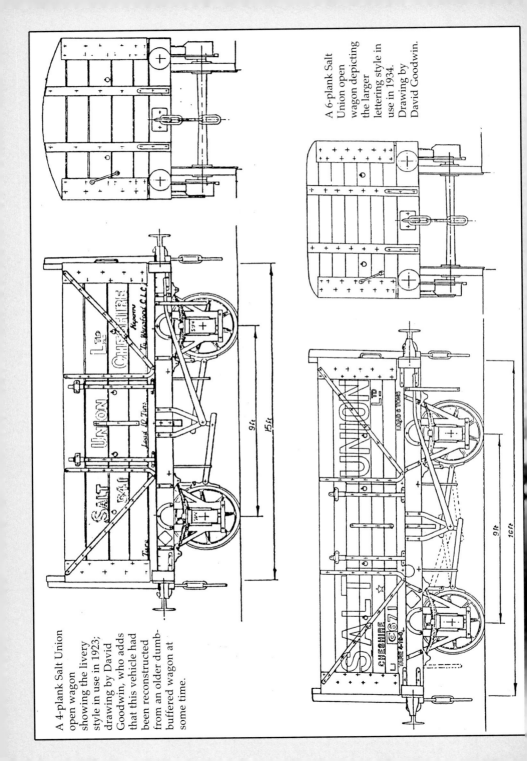

A 4-plank Salt Union open wagon showing the livery style in use in 1923; drawing by David Goodwin, who adds that this vehicle had been reconstructed from an older dumb-buffered wagon at some time.

A 6-plank Salt Union open wagon depicting the larger lettering style in use in 1934. Drawing by David Goodwin.

With the introduction of the new timetable in September 1929, as there was no longer a passenger engine stationed at Winsford, it was arranged so that all the goods trains now started and finished at Northwich, thus enabling the little engine shed at Winsford to close. The passenger service now consisted of eight trains each way on weekdays with an extra working on Saturdays. The first and last trains now started and finished at Northwich except that on Saturday nights the last train returned empty stock to Northwich. There was also the traditional Saturday lunchtime run through to Northwich, otherwise all other trains terminated at Cuddington. With one minor exception, this service remained in force up to 31st December, 1930 when the last train ran.

The railcars introduced a new livery on the branch. They were a dark brown below the waist and a light tan brown above and were lined out at the waist in primrose yellow, with one line separating the dark and light tan and a second line about two inches up into the light tan. The two body colours and the twin waist lines were continued right round each end of the coach. In addition, on the upper half of the bodysides (not the ends) there was a single vertical line on the pillars between the windows, at the side of each door and on the panel beading of the engine compartment. These yellow lines were ⅜ in. thick and had a fine red line ¹⁄₁₆ in. wide along each edge of the yellow. The vertical lines all ended at both top and bottom with an arrowhead. A special version of the CLC's armorial badge, without the gold filigree surround, was applied two per side to these steam coaches. The similar LNER railcars all had attractive names and it was a pity the CLC did not adopt the same policy; 'Vale Royal' would have been an obvious choice for No. 602. A photograph taken on the branch shows No. 602 working chimney first towards Winsford.

With regard to the goods vehicles to be seen on the branch, CLC wagons were always painted a light lead-grey colour. Until 1901 they were lettered 'CHESHIRE LINES' in small white writing, but from 1901 the large 21 in. high initials 'C L' were adopted. Most of the privately-owned wagons belonged to the Salt Union, not only for their salt traffic but also for bringing in the coal from the collieries, although some colliery-owned wagons were employed.

All the salt works north of Winsford and Over station were under the control of the Salt Union Limited which had been formed in 1888. Before this date these works had been owned by several different companies, as the names of Falk, Hickson, Deakin and Verdin testify; unfortunately no details of how their wagons were lettered are known to the author. The salt wagons were of two types, mostly open wagons but with some covered vans. The latter typically had peak roofs like a terraced house but these were a minority; far more numerous were vans with the orthodox curved roof. Livery was a dark red oxide with white lettering and black ironwork. Sometimes, chiefly on vans, the writing had black shading, and said 'SALT UNION LTD.' in one line across the wagon on the second plank down. However a later (after 1923) style had much larger lettering with 'SALT' to the left of the door and 'UNION' to the right. Another variant on vans was to have 'SALT UNION' in two lines on the left and 'UNION SALT' in two lines on the right. There were also some salt wagons still using the old name of 'FALK SALT' well into the 1920s.

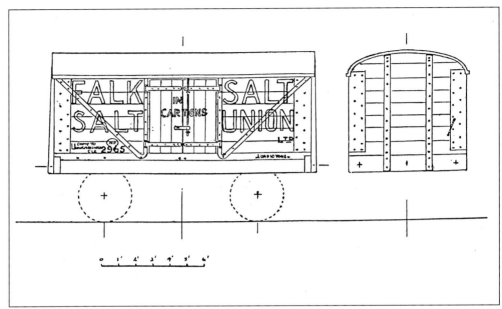

A Salt Union covered wagon with curved roof, showing the Falk Salt branding *circa* 1930.
Drawing by David Goodwin.

One of George Hamlett & Sons' covered wagons with a peak roof, *circa* 1930.

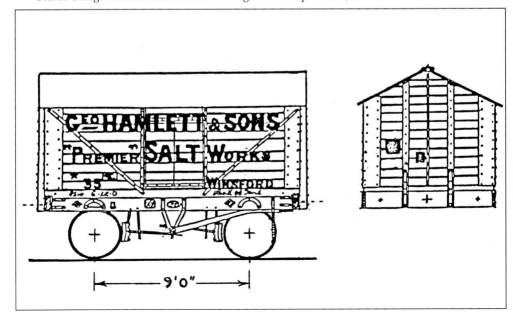

The Salt Union continued to use the brand name 'FALK' for some of its products, as shown on this peak-roofed van photographed by J.P. Richards about 1920. The livery was red oxide, with white lettering and black for the shading and all ironwork; the roof would appear to be white.

H.D. Goodwin Collection

The 'I.C.I SALT' lettering was adopted from 1940, as seen in this newly-built van of 1942; it is surprising that shaded lettering was adopted at this stage in the war, although it may only have been for this photograph of the first of the batch for publicity purposes   *Author's Collection*

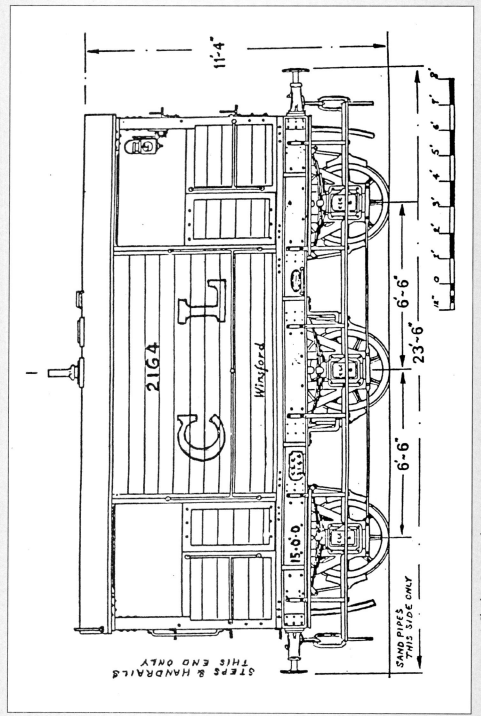

A Cheshire Lines 6-wheeled goods brake van built in 1915. No. 2164 was allocated to the Winsford branch in the 1940s.

The two salt works south of the station remained independent of the Salt Union. No information is held about Garner's wagons, but Hamlett's were lettered 'G^{EO} HAMLETT & SONS' across the top of the wagon and '"PREMIER" SALT WORKS' across the middle. The principal retailer of coal in Winsford was the local Cooperative Society and its wagons were commonplace in the goods yards at both Winsford and Whitegate. They were painted a medium grey and were strikingly lettered 'COOPERATIVE' diagonally across the wagon side from bottom left to top right in white letters, shaded black. The words 'WINSFORD INDUSTRIAL' were in smaller characters in two lines at the top left with 'SOCIETY LIMITED' in two lines in the bottom right corner. Hamlett's wagons were also medium grey with white lettering and black shading; all body ironwork and roofing was painted black.

In later years the Imperial Chemical Industries Ltd (ICI) salt wagons were painted a cherry red with white lettering. The large initials 'I C I' covered the top three planks and were additionally shaded in black. The ICI had taken over the Salt Union in 1937 but it was 1940 before the new lettering was first applied. It should also be mentioned that as from 12th January, 1930 the CLC ceased to operate its own goods stock, all the wagons being sold to the LMS and LNER although it took several years for them all to be re-lettered. The CLC continued to operate its own goods brake vans and service stock (such as ballast trucks), as well as its own passenger carriages and other coaching stock (such as horse boxes) until Nationalisation in 1948.

Mention of the CLC goods brake vans reminds me that they used to be branded with the name of the home depôt at which they were stationed and one brake van was known to have carried 'Winsford' on its sides in the 1940s; that was No. 2164, one of the six-wheeled vans with a vestibule entrance at each end built in 1915. Guard's vans branded 'Northwich' included Nos. 11, 1656 and 4463.

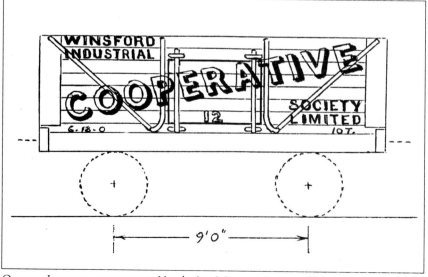

Open coal wagons were operated by the local Co-operative Society for retail distribution

The Catsclough Crossing keeper, the redoubtable Mrs Furbur, stands by the wicket gate outside her ground frame cabin about 1920. The diamond shaped linesman's board is hung to show its white side, which indicates that the signals are all in working order. If any fault had been found, then the board would have been turned round to show the red side.   *Trevor Booth*

Chapter Seven

The End of the Line for Passengers

The introduction of the steam coach to the branch passenger workings brought about economies worth some £1,000 per year, but this was not enough to stem the loss being made on these workings which had been rising considerably since 1923 due to competition on the roads. Northwich station was ¾ mile away from the town centre; the bus went direct and there was no changing at Cuddington to contend with. It was not surprising that in 1930 the CLC announced that it was proposing to discontinue its branch passenger service as soon as arrangements could be made to provide an adequate substitute omnibus service. The North Western Road Car Co. agreed to put on a new bus service between Winsford and Cuddington via Whitegate, and also to extend its existing direct route from Winsford to Northwich from the town centre to the railway station. As a result it was announced that passenger trains would be withdrawn on and from 1st January, 1931.

In its defence the CLC quoted at the time that the cost of providing the service in 1929 had been £3,587 whilst the passenger receipts at the two stations on the branch amounted to £1,951 (£3,589 in 1923). Of this, the proportion of the bookings attributable to the branch line only was £1,159 in 1929.

The replacement service put on by North Western was far more lavish than that provided by the CLC, with 14 buses each way on weekdays and, what is more, no less than nine on Sundays. Further, this increased service was maintained and had actually risen to 16 weekdays plus one extra on Saturdays and 11 on Sundays by May 1939. However, the bus journey could take up to 28 minutes, compared with 17 by train.

Nevertheless there were strong objections and the Winsford Urban District Council, as successor to the Local Board, instructed solicitors once again to apply to the Court of the Railway and Canal Commission. The hearing took place on 22nd and 23rd July, 1931. Witnesses in the shape of local residents gave evidence of hardship caused by the withdrawal of trains and the inconvenience of the replacement road service. Counsel for the applicants said that the Order granted in 1891 had clearly been breached and asked for a new Order inflicting penalties on the Committee as well as enforcing them to re-instate the passenger service forthwith.

A witness for the Committee gave evidence of the loss the railway had been making. Passenger receipts, excluding season tickets, apportioned for the branch had fallen from £1,706 in 1924 to £809 in 1930. Season tickets in 1930 had brought in an extra £37 compared with £117 in 1924. The number of passengers using the branch was 99,339 in 1924 and had dropped to 68,170 in 1930. The cost of providing the passenger service had averaged about £5,000 per annum for the years 1924 to 1927, was about £4,700 in 1928 and had been cut to £4,200 (with the use of the steamcoach for five months) in 1929. With a full year's use of the railcar the cost in 1930 had been further reduced to around £3,700. To this should be added £1,100 for part of the cost of maintaining the way and works

CHESHIRE LINES RAILWAY

CLOSING OF THE

WINSFORD BRANCH FOR PASSENGER TRAFFIC

On and from

THURSDAY, JANUARY 1st, 1931

THE PASSENGER TRAIN SERVICE

between

WINSFORD & OVER AND CUDDINGTON

WILL BE WITHDRAWN and

Winsford & Over and Whitegate Stations

will be closed for Passenger Traffic.

From that date an Omnibus Service will be provided by the North-Western Road Car Company between Winsford & Over, Whitegate and Cuddington to connect at Cuddington Station with the Rail Services run by the Cheshire Lines Railway on the Manchester-Chester line.

This road service will provide more frequent services than the existing Passenger Train Service on the Branch line.

It has been arranged that the existing half-hourly service run by the North-Western Road Car Company between Winsford & Over and Northwich Town shall be extended to serve Northwich Station, Cheshire Lines Railway.

Owners of unexpired return halves of Railway Tickets available over the Winsford Branch will be permitted to travel on their return journey within the period of availability of their tickets on the Omnibuses of the North-Western Road Car Company between Cuddington, Whitegate, and Winsford & Over.

PARCELS AND MISCELLANEOUS TRAFFIC.

Winsford & Over and Whitegate Stations will continue to deal with parcels and miscellaneous traffic, also horses, cattle, and other livestock, as at present.

GOODS, MINERAL AND LIVESTOCK TRAFFIC.

There will be no change in regard to the handling of goods, mineral and livestock traffic.

Winsford & Over and Whitegate Stations will continue to deal with these traffics as at present.

BUS SERVICE. JANUARY 1st, 1931.

WEEK DAYS.

		a.m.	a.m.	a.m.	p.m.	p.m.	p.m.	p.m.	p.m.	p.m.	p.m.
CUDDINGTON	dep.	7 5	8 45	10 50	12 5	1 15	2 0	3 5	3 55	4 50	5 52
WINSFORD	arr.	7 23	9 8	11 13	12 25	1 38	2 23	3 28	4 18	5 13	6 15

		a.m.	a.m.	a.m.	p.m.	p.m.	p.m.	p.m.	p.m.	p.m.	p.m.
WINSFORD	dep.	7 30	9 10	11 13	12 25	1 38	2 30	3 28	4 20	5 15	6 15
CUDDINGTON	arr.	7 53	9 33	11 35	12 50	2 0	2 53	3 50	4 43	5 38	6 35

		p.m.	p.m.	p.m.	p.m.	p.m.	p.m.	p.m.
CUDDINGTON	dep.	7 5	7 20	8 0	8 15	9 15	10 0	10 50
WINSFORD	arr.	7 28	7 43	8 23	8 38	9 38	10 22	11 13

		p.m.	p.m.	p.m.	p.m.	p.m.
WINSFORD	dep.	7 28	7 45	8 38	9 38	10 23
CUDDINGTON	arr.	7 50	8 8	9 0	10 0	10 46

SUNDAYS.

		p.m.	p.m.	p.m.	p.m.	p.m.	p.m.	p.m.	p.m.	p.m.
CUDDINGTON	dep.	2 0	3 5	3 55	4 50	5 52	7 5	8 0	9 15	10 0
WINSFORD	arr.	2 23	3 28	4 18	5 13	6 15	7 28	8 23	9 38	10 22

		p.m.	p.m.	p.m.	p.m.	p.m.	p.m.	p.m.	p.m.	p.m.
WINSFORD	dep.	2 30	3 28	4 20	5 15	6 15	7 28	8 38	9 38	10 23
CUDDINGTON	arr.	2 53	3 50	4 43	5 38	6 35	7 50	9 0	10 0	10 45

Central Station, Liverpool.
nw)

B. T. BURGOYNE.
Manager.

A view of Whitegate, taken from the road bridge about 1920. There are wagons left standing on the loop just beyond the signal cabin; the loop was not used for passing trains.

M. Thompson

apportioned to the passenger service. Counsel for the Committee argued that the Commission had no power to force the railway to continue making a loss in excess of £4,000 per annum.

After due deliberation the Court unanimously agreed with the Committee's case and discharged the Order of 1891 as 'a mistake in law'. Note that in court the CLC had stated the cost of the passenger service in 1929 was about £4,200 whereas just before closure it quoted £3,587. Also dividing the receipts by the number of passengers gives an average fare of 4.12d. in 1924 and of only 2.85d. in 1930. One would have expected counsel for the Council to have challenged these figures. One fact is clear, that the average number of passengers using each train had been reduced from just under 24 in 1924 to less than 14 per train in 1930.

The following figures for the annual number of passenger journeys made on the Winsford & Over branch were given in evidence by Sydney Burgoyne, the Manager of the Cheshire Lines, to the Court of the Railway and Canal Commission in July 1931:

1924	99,339	1926	65,953	1928	67,133	1930	68,170
1925	75,889	1927	65,515	1929	65,207		

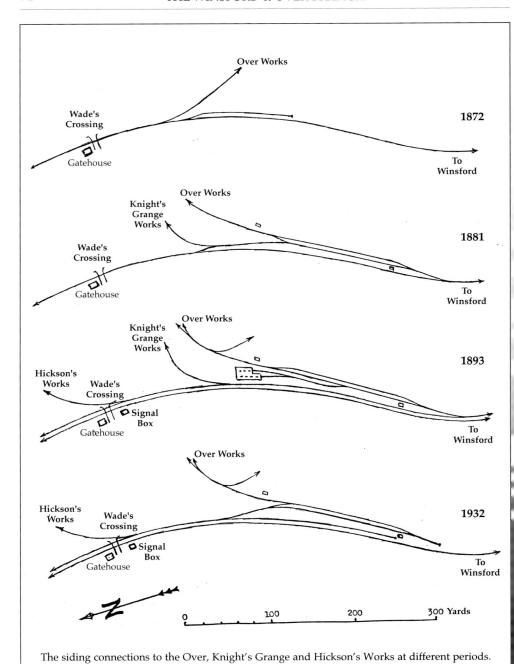

The siding connections to the Over, Knight's Grange and Hickson's Works at different periods.

Chapter Eight

The Winsford Salt Works

Prior to the coming of the railway most of the output of the salt works in the town was taken away on the River Weaver. Separate figures for the annual traffic in salt from just Winsford alone, carried by the Weaver Navigation, are available until 1880. Those for five sample years, each ending 31st March, are:-

1758	1800	1846	1873	1880	
1,055	44,384	229,611	639,054	794,054	tons

It was this sort of growth in traffic that encouraged the LNWR and the CLC to build their branches to the salt works on each side of the river. For the years after 1880 only the total tonnage of salt carried on the whole of the Weaver is available, which includes the output from Northwich as well as Winsford. This shows that in the 12 years following 1881 the salt traffic fell by 45 per cent, attributable to the competition from the railways. If the Winsford traffic alone fell by the same proportion it would mean that 357,671 tons of salt annually had been transferred to the railways by 1893, which equates to 165 wagon loads at 7 tons each for every weekday. This of course was shared between the LNWR and the CLC, and allowing for rather more salt works on the LNWR side of the river by fixing the CLC's share at 40 per cent, this produces an average of 16 salt wagons for each of the CLC's four daily goods trains.

In addition there was a considerable volume of coal carried to the salt works. On average it required one ton of coal to make four tons of coarse salt by the open pan method, and up to 2½ tons of coal if fine salt was being produced. The black smoke that bellowed out of the numerous chimneys of the salt works was testimony to the amount of coal being consumed. In the 12 months to March 1846 the Weaver Navigation brought in 59,014 tons just to Winsford alone, and one would expect this figure to have more than doubled by 1873. This river-borne traffic was absolutely decimated by the competition of the new railways; the annual tonnage fell by no less than 87 per cent in the 12 years to 1893, having already dropped by 22 per cent in the previous ten years. This equates to 59 wagons daily at 7 tons each by 1893, with the CLC share at a possible 40 per cent working out at 24 wagons of coal, or six per train. Even though these figures are only an approximation they indicate why the CLC found it necessary to operate four daily goods trains, soon increased to five, to and from Winsford at this period.

There were over a dozen different salt works on the west bank of the Weaver, many with their own private railway systems connected to the CLC, and from 1888 nine of them were included in that new combine called the Salt Union Limited. The pre-1888 situation is complicated by many of the companies then owning more than one works, some of them on the other side of the river. It is easier to mention each works on a geographical basis, starting at the south end nearest the town centre, and working northwards along the west bank of the Weaver.

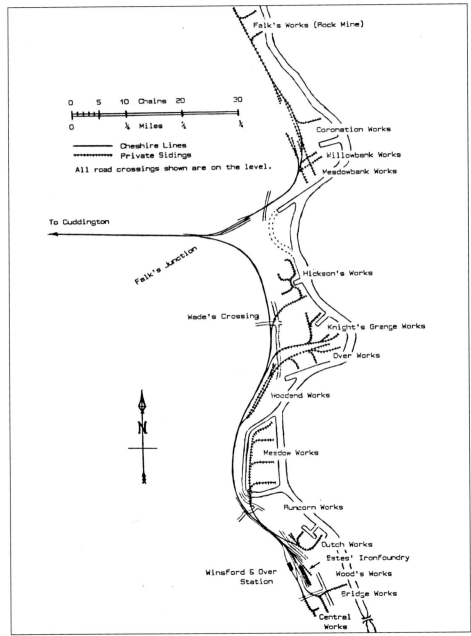

The numerous salt works served by the CLC extended for nearly 1½ miles along the west bank of the River Weaver.

The Central Salt Works, also known as the Premier Works, was immediately south of Winsford and Over station, and was the only one on the CLC side which was not alongside the river. It was owned by George Hamlett and Sons, who also had interests in Stafford, and is not shown on the first edition OS map of 1872 but was evidently established in the next few years. The CLC connection was put in about 1879 or shortly after, and later another siding was laid into the works. Hamlett's did not join the Salt Union but remained independent until 1950 when taken over by Amasol Ltd. The Central Works was actually the last traditional open pan works to remain in Winsford, finally closing in 1961.

Just north of Winsford Bridge, to the south-east of the station, stood the Bridge Salt Works of J. Garner & Co. This is marked on the 1872 survey but was not rail connected until sometime in the 1880s. Garner's never joined the Salt Union and the works closed in 1928 or 1929, but the site and also the firm's boats were subsequently acquired by the Salt Union. The siding remained, and later in 1929 was leased to the Winsford Urban District Council. In 1938 it is shown as being used by the Winsford Gas Co. and in 1944 it is marked as 'Council Road'. Any coal or coke supplies would have to have been carted across the High Street to reach the town gas works, which was not rail connected. The siding was closed in 1961, the last customer being the National Coal Board. Neither Hamlett's nor Garner's ever owned a shunting engine.

Proceeding north, the next place was Wood's Winsford Salt Works, immediately east of the station. This is believed to have been the oldest salt works in Winsford. Originally owned by Thomas Patten, Isaac Wood became the proprietor in 1744. Wood also carried on a thriving business on the Weaver, taking 85 per cent of the river traffic in 1760, but later most of the salt firms operated their own boat fleets. Wood's Works remained loyal to the river and was never rail connected, although some supplies could have been carted the short distance to or from the station yard. Never part of the Salt Union, the works had closed down by 1930.

Adjacent to the CLC's engine shed stood the Dutch Salt Works, and this did have its own rail system which was joined to the main line (by the station signal box) right from the branch opening in 1870. The owner was Richard Evans & Sons of Haydock, better known as colliery proprietors in the St Helens area. Just prior to 1888 the ownership of the Dutch Works, and also two other salt works on the east bank of the Weaver, was transferred to Joseph Evans, one of the sons, in order to facilitate the sale of Evans' salt interests to the Salt Union. The rail connection seems to have been closed by 1904 although the works is still shown on the 1913 edition OS map, but not on the 1930 map. It is marked as dismantled in a list of 1913.

The Runcorn Salt Works is the next one north, and was owned by the Cheshire Amalgamated Salt Works Limited, whose main establishment was on the LNWR side of the Weaver, and who also owned works at Wheelock, Malkin's Bank, Whitehall and Northwich. The company was formed in 1865 by combining the firm of James Blackwell with that of John Kay & Son. Christopher Kay was the Managing Director when the company sold out to the Salt Union in 1888. There is no evidence of any rail connection to the Runcorn Works, however there was a siding alongside the CLC line opposite the works which was put in in 1870 but was marked as Verdin & Sons' Siding in 1881. This works had also been dismantled by 1913.

The Meadow Salt Works of Joseph Verdin & Sons, on a man-made island in the river, has previously been mentioned when it was rail connected by a swing bridge in 1876. On the 1893 plan it is marked as the Wharton Salt Works and it was also known as the Whartonmeadow and the Island Works, but Meadow is the more familiar name. Verdin's, first established in Winsford in 1863, also owned works on the LNWR side of the river, another further north on the CLC side, and others at Marston, Middlewich and Northwich, and was the largest of the Winsford salt firms to join the Salt Union in 1888; they claimed in 1881 to own 576 railway wagons and 27 railway vans. In later years a portion of the Meadow Works became the central workshops for the Salt Union (and ICI) in Winsford, and salt production here had ceased by the mid-1930s. The rail connection was taken out of use on 1st May, 1965 following the closure of the workshops.

The Woodend Salt Works is one about which little is known. It is not shown on the 1872 survey but is depicted on the 1893 plan. There was then no internal rail system but the private lines of Deakin's Over Works ran right alongside. However, a siding connection to the works is referred to in 1916. The site had been cleared by 1930, but no owner has been traced although it would appear to be on Salt Union land. The Over Salt Works of George Deakin Ltd had a simple siding connection with the CLC facing towards Cuddington according to the 1872 map, but by 1881 the internal rail system was much more complex with a completely new CLC connection, which now faced Winsford station. The 1893 plan depicted a two-road engine shed next to the CLC line. Deakin's also owned works on the LNWR side of the valley and duly sold out to the Salt Union in 1888. In 1931, or just after, the CLC connection was changed yet again, reverting more or less to the form it had in 1872. The sidings were still in use in 1956 but the Over Works had closed before the end of the Meadow Works in 1965. A Jubilee Works given in a 1920s list is believed to have been an alternative name for this salt works, whilst a CLC plan of 1944 called it the Wade Works.

Continuing north, the Knight's Grange Salt Works existed in 1872 but was not rail connected until about 1877 and by 1881 had its own internal system with the CLC connection facing towards Winsford. Owned by Joseph Verdin & Sons, and thus becoming Salt Union in 1888, it was also known as the Dairy Works. The term 'dairy' was used to describe a particularly fine grade of salt. This works seems to have closed about 1930 or just after.

Hickson's Salt Works was owned by William and Robert Hickson who rather confusingly referred to it as the Knight's Grange Works. No rail connection is shown on the first edition OS map of 1872 but one had been provided by 1881, facing towards Winsford. Taken over by the Salt Union in 1888, this works is believed to have closed in the late 1920s. There were 20 pans in 1888, reduced to six (with only two in use) by 1913. Until 1876 the Ravenhead Colliery Co. of St Helens owned the Knight's Grange Salt Works, but unfortunately it is not known whether this applied to Verdin's or to the Hickson's works of that name. A guess, for what it is worth, is that it was Verdin's because in the 1870s the CLC used the term Verdin's Siding only for that serving the Meadow Works, suggesting that Joseph Verdin & Sons might not have been the original owner of the Knight's Grange Works.

The Meadowbank Works of the Salt Union between 1919 and 1932, looking north-east, with the CLC tracks in the foreground. Performing the shunting is one of the Falcon Engine & Car Works locomotives, probably *Newbridge*. The tall building on the extreme right is the corner of the Vacuum Plant. *Author's Collection*

The Meadowbank Salt Works (sometimes shown as Meadow Bank) of the Falk Salt Co. was connected to the CLC branch from Falk's Junction on 18th June, 1873 at a cost of £480, but there was an internal rail system in the works shown on the 1872 map, so there was probably an earlier connection dating from 1870. Falk Salt was established in Winsford in 1841 by Herman Eugen Falk, originally and until 1848 in partnership with his elder brother. About half a mile further north was the Rock Salt Mine, which was acquired by H.E. Falk before 1851 but does not appear to have been rail connected before it closed about 1890. Following the death of his first wife in 1851, Falk had leased the Meadowbank Works and the mine to his brother-in-law John Thompson, until 1856. On its formation in 1888 the Salt Union Ltd, as well as taking over the Meadowbank Works and Rock Mine from H.E. Falk, also acquired the Willowbank Salt Works from Henry Ingram Thompson and a lease of the same from John Thompson, both of whom are shown as also having a salt works at Witton. The Willowbank Works seems to have been on the same general site as the Meadowbank Works. The whole Meadow Bank area was considerably developed by the Salt Union after 1888.

In 1889 the Salt Union (SU) had purchased a works at Over (and thus on the west bank) from the Runcorn Soap and Alkali Co., the exact location of which is not known. Then in 1898 the SU had opened a new soap works at Meadow Bank, presumably a replacement for the previous works. Next came a power plant that provided electricity for all the SU works in Winsford. It was shown on a plan of 1909 as the Coronation Works so presumably it dated from 1902. This was followed by the opening of the Vacuum Plant in 1905, which was the first attempt to produce salt from brine anywhere other than by the open pan method. It relied on much lower temperatures being required for evaporation

Looking north-east over the Weaver from a point about 530 yards from Winsford & Over station *circa* 1910. The CLC double-tracked line is in the foreground with the Meadow Salt Works at centre and right just across the river. In middle distance, on the left bank, is the Woodend Works, whilst on the opposite bank on the right is the Wharton Lodge (or Dudley) Works. Further downstream, in the centre distance, is the Lycett (Railway & River) Works.   *Author's Collection*

Another view of the salt works taken around 1910; this time the photographer is standing some 730 yards north of Winsford station looking due east. The locomotive on the CLC main line is Great Central No. 379, a double framed Sacré 0-6-0 of class '6A', whilst the train of 'Bolsover' coal wagons is standing on the Over Works siding. The wagon on the extreme left is just about where the 1888 collision took place, with the end of the Woodend Works above. Across the river, at left and centre, is the Wharton Lodge Works, with the Uploont Works on the right. On the distant skyline is the Wharton Works with the Cheshire Amalgamated Works on the extreme left.   *John Ryan Collection/J.A. Peden C8153*

of the brine in a near vacuum, and used exhaust steam from the adjacent power plant for the evaporators.

The Rock Mine was reopened in 1928, rather confusingly being called Falk's Works, and this time it was provided with a rail connection. There was an engine shed at the north end of the main Meadowbank Works where the line to the mine went off. Even more confusing are the names given to some of the Salt Union sidings. Listed in 1904 and until 1927 were a Meadow Bank Works, a Soap Works and a Willow Bank Works. From 1929 the list had changed to Meadow Bank Works, Falk's Works (opened 1928) and Vacuum Plant (opened 1905). It is thought that Willow Bank could be an alternative name for the Vacuum Plant, perhaps because the plant was built on the site of the old Willowbank Works. In ICI days, after 1938, a Factory Works made an appearance but as Meadowbank Works had now dropped out it is presumed that this was yet another alternative name. The Coronation Works (power plant?) closed about 1957 and the Vacuum Plant in 1964, but the Rock Mine is still in production although rail traffic finally ceased on 13th March, 1967 and all the track was taken up the following year.

There is one other private siding that needs to be mentioned, even though it had nothing to do with the salt industry. J. Bates & Sons had an iron foundry between New Road and the east side of Winsford and Over station, and their siding was provided in 1926 or 1927 by the simple expedient of extending the turntable road across the station forecourt into the foundry yard. Contemporary plans of the siding mark the turntable still in position but it had not been used for many years, at least since 1907 if not earlier. The pit had probably been filled in and later plans do not show any turntable here. The siding was still listed in 1956, with the title of the firm changed to J. Bates & Son Ltd, and closed around 1958, when Bates & Son moved to a new site.

A revolutionary change took place in the salt industry in 1888 by the formation of the Salt Union Limited, which acquired the majority of the Winsford salt works in its first year. Originally proposed by H.E. Falk in 1886, the agreement to form the new combine was taken at a meeting at the Adelphi Hotel in Liverpool on 5th July and the new company was registered on 8th October, 1888. Altogether 66 different vendors throughout the country transferred property, brine rights and leases to the SU. There were six representatives of Winsford salt firms on the original Board of 14 Directors, including two sons of Joseph Verdin (who had died in 1881) - young Joseph (knighted in 1897) and William Henry - plus George Henry Deakin, Christopher Kay and Herman John Falk (son of H.E.). Other Directors were financiers from the City with no connection with the salt industry, of whom Lord Thurlow was Chairman, Charles William Mills was from the bankers Glyn, Mills, Currie & Co. and Walter Robinson was also a Director (and later Deputy Chairman) of the Great Western Railway.

Besides a large number (over 3,000) of rail wagons the Salt Union on its formation also acquired the boat fleets of the companies it had taken over. H.E. Falk had built the first steam barge on the Weaver in 1863, whilst Robert Verdin (one of the sons, who died in 1887) had introduced the steam winch to Winsford about the same time. Many of the boats were built in the town, six of the salt firms having their own dockyards including Deakin's, Falk's and Verdin's. During World War I two of the Winsford steam barges, the *Albion* and the *Dolphin*, were commandeered by the Royal Navy and sent to Scapa Flow. When Garner's Bridge Salt Works closed down in 1928-29 their boats were added to the SU fleet. In later years several of these steam packets were converted to motor barges.

W.H. Verdin was held in particularly high esteem by Winsfordians. He sponsored the town's Technical School, opened in 1895 and now part of the Verdin Comprehensive, and also the Public Library of 1888. This is now a reference library for schools. He also donated the building of the Albert Infirmary in 1898, which is now demolished leaving Winsford today without any hospital. Other benefactors to the town included the Weaver Navigation which provided the Christ Church on the High Street, and Sir John Brunner who paid for the Guildhall.

Although Brunner, Mond & Co. became shareholders they never joined the Union, and they extracted themselves a considerable proportion of the brine used in the chemical industry, with a disastrous effect on the Salt Union revenues. Coupled with an over-capitalisation and bad management policies, the new Union was soon in trouble, causing an irreparable split in the Board. From a bright first year's results in 1889, profits quickly tumbled by a rate of around 15 per cent each year so that in 1898 a loss was made. All the original Directors except H.J. Falk had by now resigned and control of the company had passed into the hands of Liverpool merchants.

Gradually the Salt Union recovered, a small profit being recorded each year from 1900 to 1915, followed by better (but still moderate) results from 1916 onwards. The best year was 1920 with a net profit of around £275,000, compared with the first year's high spot of £320,000, on a capital of £4,000,000.

Between 1925 and 1927 the Salt Union regrouped the various Winsford works into three administrative units, first shown in the November 1927 list of sidings in a CLC handbook. The South Works was spread over both sides of the river; on the CLC side it included Hickson's, Knight's Grange, Over and Meadow Works. The East Works was exclusively on the east (LNWR) side of the Weaver. The third new unit, the West Works, was entirely on the CLC side and comprised the Meadowbank, Coronation and Falk's Works and the Vacuum Plant.

Brunner, Mond & Co., established at Winnington in 1873 and Limited from 1881, joined forces with two other chemical firms to form Imperial Chemical Industries Ltd in December 1926, and a controlling interest was acquired in the Salt Union from March 1937. H.J. Falk had remained a Director from the beginning to the end, having been Deputy Chairman since 1908. Trading under the Salt Union name continued until 28th March, 1940 when a new company - ICI (Salt) Ltd - took over. This was disbanded at the end of 1942 and the Salt Division of ICI was formed on 1st January, 1943. Eighteen years later this division was absorbed into the Alkali Division, which in turn amalgamated with the General Chemicals Division to form the new Mond Division on 1st January, 1964. Subsequent changes, after the railway had closed, do not really concern us except to mention that in May 1992 ICI sold the Rock Mine at Winsford to a consortium which took as its new name the Salt Union Ltd. The mine was, as mentioned, the only one of the once numerous salt works left in Winsford.

Chapter Nine

The Works' Shunting Engines

A number of industrial locomotives were employed on shunting duties around the various salt works on both sides of the river. As the many sidings abounded in sharp curves, all the engines except one were small four-wheeled designs, usually with a saddle tank over the boiler. Being in the common ownership of the Salt Union, and later ICI, they were frequently exchanged between the different works (using CLC metals), and sometimes got transferred across the river and back again, so it is necessary to mention all the locomotives even though it is probable that a few of them never operated regularly on the CLC side. However they all had to come to the central workshops at the Meadow Works when repairs were needed, and some came here to be cut-up for scrap when considered beyond repair.

The earliest known engine was *George Deakin*, a saddle tank with 10 in. by 16 in. outside cylinders and built by the Wigan firm of J. Scarisbrick Walker & Bros (No. 334) about 1873 for G.B. Deakin, later George Deakin Ltd, and became Salt Union property in 1888. She is believed to have been the only engine built at the Globe Foundry in Wigan, as the order was booked about 1872 and the foundry was badly damaged on 2nd August, 1873. As a result, the firm moved to the Pagefield Ironworks in Wigan, and shortly afterwards changed its title to Walker Bros. In later life, after March 1943, this engine was transferred to the ICI works at Weston Point, Runcorn, before being sold to the Britannia Scrap Metal Co. of Ditton in late 1951 or early 1952. After being hired-out to Corn Products Ltd in Trafford Park, Manchester for several months, she was scrapped at Ditton in July 1953. In her last few years she ran without her nameplates.

A sister locomotive was *Bostock*, built by Walker Bros about 1881. The pre-1888 ownership is not certain but George Deakin Ltd had a Bostock Salt Works on the east bank. Walker Bros received an order (No. 2021) in August 1880 for a 10 in. by 16 in. tank engine, customer not known, but is likely to be this engine. At some time after 1922 she was transferred to the Salt Union's Port Clarence Works (Co. Durham) and after the last war turned up during the construction of the Meaford Power Station before moving on to the Sully (Glam.) Works of the Distillers Co., being broken up about 1949.

The oldest known shunting engine at Winsford was *Ant*, a little well tank with 10 in. by 18 in. outside cylinders and 2 ft 6 in. wheels, built by James Cross at St Helens around 1866 for Richard Evans & Sons, and which came to Winsford some time before April 1888 after possibly first working at Haydock. After passing to the Salt Union she remained at Winsford until she was cut-up in 1931. There was a sister locomotive at Haydock named *Bee* which it is believed may have deputised at Winsford on the odd occasion that *Ant* returned to Haydock for repairs in pre-1888 days.

Cheshire was a small saddle tank with inclined 10 in. by 18 in. outside cylinders and 3 ft 0 in. wheels built by S. Lewin of Poole (No. 606) in 1875 for

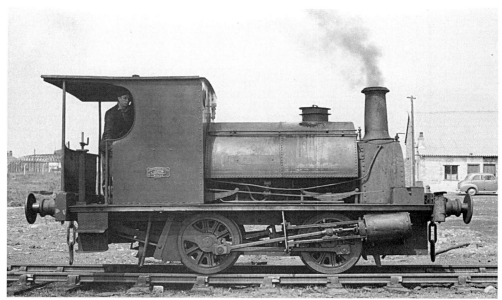

An un-named locomotive, formerly *George Deakin*, seen in later years at Widnes in August 1951. This is the only known engine to be built by the Wigan firm of J. Scarisbrick Walker & Brothers, and worked in the Winsford salt works from 1873 until 1943.   *Frank Jones*

The locomotive *Cheshire* built in 1875 by Stephen Lewin of the Poole Foundry for the Cheshire Amalgamated Salt Works Ltd in Winsford, and passed to the Salt Union Ltd in 1888. The name was painted on the side tank in place of the builder's plate shown.   *The Engineer*

the Cheshire Amalgamated Salt Works Ltd, whose main works were on the LNWR side of the Weaver. She has been associated with the Runcorn Works on the CLC side but this is unlikely as this works is not known to have had a rail system. She was transferred by the Salt Union to their South Durham Works in 1907, by which time she had been renamed *Wharton*, possibly in 1881 when a new boiler was fitted. She lasted until 1948 when she was cut-up for scrap by Thos W. Ward at Middlesbrough.

Northwich was another outside-cylindered saddle tank, built by the Falcon Engine & Car Works at Loughborough in 1884 for Joseph Verdin & Sons, and came to the Salt Union in 1888. Mostly associated with the SU mine at Marston, she was recalled locally as having worked at Winsford. In 1928 she was transferred by the SU to their Stoke Works in Worcestershire. Another Falcon engine was *Newbridge*, building date unknown but probably also new to Verdin's as they owned the Newbridge Works on the east bank of the Weaver. This engine also moved to the Stoke Works, but not until February 1947. A third Falcon-built engine was *Winsford*, probably ordered by Verdin's but delivered new (No. 117) to the Salt Union in 1889. This engine was transferred away from Winsford to the Port Clarence Works at an unknown date, but before 1943.

There was a most curious looking saddle tank engine named *Liverton* which used to shunt at the Meadowbank Works. She was built by Robey & Co. of Lincoln (No. 1931) in 1870 for the Liverton Iron Stone Mines at Loftus and had 11½ in. by 21 in. inside cylinders, 3 ft 6 in. wheels and a marine type firebox placed over the rear crank-axle. Later she was with the Salt Union at their South Durham Works at Haverton Hill, not very far from Loftus, and was transferred to Winsford in August 1907. At some date she had been involved in a collision with a North Eastern (NER) locomotive and had been repaired by the NER, which is why she had an NER-style chimney and dome in her later years. The date of her disposal or scrapping is unknown but was perhaps about 1930.

The above account is all that is known about the earlier (pre-1916) locomotives but there may well have been others; surely Falk's had an engine, for instance?

Although the finances of the Salt Union had considerably improved from 1916 onwards, no new locomotives were ever purchased, not even in ICI days, for use at Winsford but another seven steam and two diesel engines were acquired second-hand. The next to arrive was *Avon*, the only six-wheeler to be employed in the salt works. A saddle tank with 13 in. by 20 in. outside cylinders and 3 ft 6½ in. wheels, she had been built by Fox, Walker of Bristol (No. 328) in 1877 for the Nailsea Coal Co. and subsequently was acquired by the Droitwich Salt Co. Ltd. This company was one of those taken over by the Salt Union in 1888 which transferred the locomotive first to their Stoke Works, and then about 1923 to Winsford. She did not stay long, being disposed of in 1930 and subsequently turned up with William Jones of Greenwich, a dealer in second-hand locomotives.

Another engine to come from the Stoke Works, in 1925, was *Vengeance* built by Peckett & Sons of Bristol (No. 1492) in 1917 for the Royal Arsenal at Woolwich with 14 in. by 20 in. outside cylinders and 3 ft 2½ in. wheels. She was

A Falcon locomotive, *Northwich*, new to Joseph Verdin & Sons in 1884. Note the Salt Union wagon with the old-style small lettering, in use until about 1922.

Author's Collection

The Salt Union's locomotive *Winsford*, built by the Falcon Engine & Car Works in 1889, looking very smart when photographed on 19th June, 1934. Note the canvas sheet which could be drawn across the open back of the cab in wet weather.   *Derek Stoyel 204*

Salt Union No. 1 *Liverton*, an unusual looking inside cylinder saddle tank locomotive, built by Robey & Co. of Lincoln in 1870. Photographed at the Meadowbank (Falk's) Works about 1920.
                    Author's Collection

Victoria was a neat little patent side tank built by Fletcher, Jennings in 1882; the patent was in the way the valve motion was driven from the front axle. It is seen at Winsford about 1948.

Frank Jones

Seen shunting at the West (Falk's) Works of ICI on 21st August, 1954 is this 1942-built Bagnall with the nameplate *R.O.F. 10. No. 3.* She had been sent to Winsford by the Ministry of Supply.

Alex Appleton

noted working on the CLC side of the Weaver in March 1943 and again in September 1948, and was broken up for scrap about 1957. A third Bristol-built engine transferred from Stoke Works around this time (by 1930) was *Annie*, built by Fox, Walker (No. 185) in 1875. She is believed to have been scrapped about 1930. Like the other Bristol locomotives, she had a saddle tank and outside cylinders.

Victoria was a neat Fletcher, Jennings (No. 181) patent side tank with 12 in. by 20 in. outside cylinders built at Lowca, Whitehaven in 1882 for the Parkside Mining Co. of Frizington in Cumberland. She came to Winsford after the mines closed about 1926. The name was applied in large letters on the side tanks instead of the usual nameplates. Various parts, but not the boiler, were noted at the Meadow Works in October 1953 but there was nothing left in August 1954.

The remaining engines came in ICI days. *R.O.F. 10 No. 3* was built in Stafford by W.G. Bagnall & Co. (No. 2676) in 1942 and sent new to the Royal Ordnance Factory at Rearsby in Leicestershire. She was transferred to Winsford in 1944 by the Ministry of Supply to work at Meadowbank as a new shaft had been sunk during the war at the Rock Mine. She was purchased from the Ministry after the war ended and was noted working at Meadowbank, still with her *R.O.F. 10 No. 3* plates on the saddle tank, in August 1954, but was broken up about three years later.

The next engine was *Delwyn*, yet another Bristol-built engine, this time by the Avonside Engine Co. (No. 1565), built for stock in 1908 and delivered new as *Finetta* in 1911 to the Teign Valley Granite Co. Ltd, Devon and after passing to Roads Reconstruction Ltd, went to A.R.Adams of Newport who resold her to the Glamorgan Canal Co. in 1931. Now renamed *Delwyn*, she worked at the Cardiff Basin and later at the East Dock for the Bute Docks Estate. She was purchased by ICI in 1946 from Cardiff Corporation and sent to Winsford, where she was again renamed, this time as *John L. Deuchar*. The new acquisition, another saddle tank, had 14 in. by 20 in. outside cylinders and 3 ft 3 in. wheels, and was noted working at Meadowbank in September 1948 but did not last much longer, being scrapped about 1953.

The last steam locomotive to arrive at the Winsford salt works was *Humber*, a saddle tank with 12 in. by 20 in. outside cylinders and 3 ft 2 in. wheels, built by Andrew Barclay of Kilmarnock (No. 1800) in 1923 as *Preston* for Sir William Arrol's contract on Sunderland Docks. Subsequently this engine was with Casebourne & Co. (1926) Ltd at Haverton Hill, then from 1929 at the Billingham Works of ICI, transferred in 1951 to the Port Clarence Works, and finally to Winsford in 1953 by which time she had been renamed. She only lasted here a very short time, being broken up about 1955.

And so to the two little four-wheeled diesel locomotives, both built by Rushton & Hornsby of Lincoln to their class '88DS', they came to Winsford in 1956-57 from other ICI salt works and worked at Meadowbank. One (No. 306089) was built in 1950 and came from the Weston Point Works; she was named *Richard Morris* and was sold about March 1963 to Thos W. Ward Ltd. of Sheffield, who resold her to the South Western Gas Board at Bath in February 1964. The other diesel (No. 252836) was built in 1948 and came in 1956 from the

Stoke Works. She was noted at the Meadowbank Works in August 1959 with the painted name *Robert Bennet,* but the spelling had been corrected to *Robert Bennett* by the time the engine was disposed of to the Monckton Coke & Chemicals Co. Ltd near Royston in 1967 after rail traffic ceased in March.

Mention should also be made of the underground narrow gauge system installed in the Rock Salt Mine (Falk's Works) in 1928, and replaced by dumper trucks about 1956. Of nominal two feet gauge, three 4-wheel battery-electric locomotives built by Wingrove & Rogers Ltd of Southport are known, and there may well have been at least one other. Also two narrow gauge steam locomotives were stored in the Meadow Works for more than 20 years until sold for scrap in 1936. Named *Aston* and *Gladstone,* they had come from the Connah's Quay Alkali Co. of Wepre in Flintshire, and one of them was remarkably still languishing in a Warrington scrapyard until about 1953. They probably only came to Winsford because there was ample space to keep them in store.

Gladstone, one of two narrow-gauge engines stored at the Meadow Works of the Salt Union for more than 20 years until 1936, here seen in a scrap yard in Warrington on 27th October, 1946.   *Harold D. Bowtell*

Chapter Ten

The Final Years

After the withdrawal of passenger trains on the branch for the third and final time on New Year's Day 1931, Northwich Shed found it had no use for a Sentinel steamcoach, so No. 602 was transferred to Liverpool Brunswick from where it continued to work until August 1944, being withdrawn two months later and sent to Doncaster for scrapping by the LNER. Considerable economies were now introduced into the working of the line. The double line between Falk's Junction and Winsford reverted to single track again. The middle section of the former down goods line was lifted but the remaining ends of the line were retained for access to the various sidings. A new connection (the third) was put in for the Over Works. The line was now worked under the One Engine in Steam regulations, with a key staff for the whole branch held at Winsford Junction signal box. The engine shed at Winsford, disused since September 1929, was demolished. When Whitegate box was abolished in July 1947 the cost was put at £421 and the annual saving in maintenance said to be £72; the box had been operated by a porter as required and he was redeployed so there was no saving in labour costs. It thus took six years to pay for the cost of replacing the box with ground frames.

The goods timetable for Winter 1931-32 showed weekday trains from Northwich at 7.20 am and 12.55 pm plus a third on Mondays to Fridays at 4.15 pm, returning from Winsford at 11.20 am (which ran non-stop from Whitegate to Northwich East Sidings), 4.00 pm daily and at 6.30 pm Saturdays excepted. The guard on this third train only travelled outwards from Northwich as far as Cuddington where he changed over with the guard of the 4.00 pm ex-Winsford. The engine of the 12.55 pm from Northwich, after disposal of the train at Winsford, had two hours in which to proceed to Falk's Junction to prepare outward traffic before returning to the terminus for the next train. Although passengers had been transferred to buses, parcels and other traffic (such as horses) normally handled by passenger train were still catered for on the branch. The first down goods from Northwich was shown as calling at Cuddington on Tuesdays, Thursdays and Fridays only for parcels traffic only; whilst the 6.30 pm (SX) from Winsford was allowed five minutes in Northwich station to unload parcels traffic to connect, when possible, with the 8.30 pm Northwich to Manchester before proceeding to Northwich East Sidings.

The Winter 1937-38 timetable showed few changes from 1932. The first morning departure from Northwich now ran five minutes earlier and the Mondays to Fridays departure was now at 4.50 instead of 4.15 pm, and called at Cuddington for parcels, and Whitegate for tranships. The 11.20 am from Winsford now stopped at Northwich when required to unload tranships for the 12.42 pm ex-Chester to Manchester train, and the 4.00 pm also unloaded tranships on arrival at Northwich. There was now no changing over of guards. An additional note in the timetable quoted:

An enthusiasts' special railtour train arrives at the Winsford terminus in October 1953; a class 'C13' 4-4-2T No. 67436 with an ex-Great Central push and pull set. The track in the foreground curves round to serve the gasworks siding, on the site of the former Bridge Salt Works. The backs of the station cottages can be seen on the extreme right.   *Neville Fields*

The same 1953 railtour train depicted from another angle, with Hamlett's Central Salt Works in the right distance, and Bates' Foundry on the left behind the station nameboard.

Harry Townley

Definite arrangements to be made by Chester to load Winsford cattle in fitted trucks and despatch by 4.19 pm SX passenger train to Manchester, due Cuddington 4.49, for connection at Cuddington with 5.10 pm train (4.50 ex-Northwich); also keep well in touch with Control should any alternative working be found necessary.

From time to time the occasional special excursion train had brought passengers back to the branch; the first as early as Saturday 31st January, 1931 when a football excursion ran from Winsford to Chester and return. On 17th October, 1953 an enthusiasts' chartered train, organised by the Railway Correspondence and Travel Society and entitled the 'Warrington & District Railtour', worked right into Winsford & Over station. It consisted of an ex-GCR 4-4-2T locomotive No. 67436 and an ex-GCR two-coach push and pull set. This was expected to be a last train as Winsford goods yard had closed on 1st September, British Railways having already proposed to close the branch. However a new joint arrangement was made with ICI which allowed traffic to continue for another eight years, but following the closure of Whitegate station on 4th November, 1963 the branch remained open only to serve the salt works.

From 6th September, 1948 one goods each way was deleted leaving just two trains on Mondays to Fridays with one on Saturdays. These left Northwich Sidings at 7.10 am and 1.00 pm (SX) with the returns from Winsford at 12.00 noon and 6.00 pm (SX). The first working only got back to Northwich Sidings at 1.10 pm so the two trains actually crossed in Northwich station and thus required two engines except on Saturdays. There was now no mention of any special provision for parcels traffic.

Occasionally, and by special arrangement, passengers were allowed to travel by goods train (in the guard's van) and on 21st February, 1959 a small group were able to journey in this fashion over the branch. Two years later the timetable for Summer 1961 showed the two goods trains daily on Mondays to Fridays only (none on Saturdays) and between Northwich Sidings and Falk's Junction only. Note that there was by now no regular service beyond Falk's to either the Over or the Meadow Works. The two trains could be worked by the same engine if required, the first getting back to Northwich an hour before the second was due to set off. The morning train was allowed 50 minutes at Falk's Junction to do any shunting whereas the afternoon train was given 110 minutes for this function. The long innings of the ex-GCR 0-6-0 tender engines, latterly classes 'J10' and 'J11', was drawing to a close by 1957 and ex-LMS class '4F' 0-6-0s were taking over the branch goods trains. However, with a selection of class '8F' 2-8-0s on hand it is quite possible that Northwich Shed used one of these engines from time to time, although no sightings are recorded.

In the meantime there had been a second enthusiasts' excursion train, organised by the same Society as before, this one on 26th March, 1960 being called the 'Cheshire District Railtour'. The train consisted of five ex-LMS corridor coaches, undoubtedly the only time corridor stock had traversed the branch, hauled by 2-6-0 No. 46472. This time the train stopped short of the platform although the locomotive continued into the station to run round. Shortly after, and by June 1961, the line beyond the connection to the Meadow Works was taken out of use and the official length of the branch was now shown as 5 miles 78 chains; that is 10 chains (or 220 yards) short of the station.

A second enthusiasts' railtour was run in March 1960, and is here seen entering Winsford & Over from the rear of the train of corridor stock. Rather more of the Central Salt Works can be seen as the goods shed has by now been demolished. *Rex Christiansen*

A few minutes later than the previous photograph, and the passengers have unloaded to explore the closed station whilst the engine, 2-6-0 No. 46472, runs round its train. *Rex Christiansen*

Above: Falk's Junction, looking up Ellis's Bank towards Whitegate, soon after the final closure of the line in March 1967. The tracks on the left are the main line to Winsford & Over, whilst those on the right lead to the West (Meadowbank) Works.   *Geoffrey Platt*

Left: Looking south towards Baker's Lane Occupation Crossing on 26th May, 1968, after the track had been recovered, taken about 500 yards north of Winsford station. The lane came out to join the road at the gate to the right of the furthest lamp-post (at extreme left). The branch to Verdin's Meadow Works left the CLC by this gate and crossed the road on the level just past the sharpest point in the bend.   *Tim Shuttleworth*

Below: The road approach to Whitegate station on 26th May, 1968, looking towards Falk's Junction. The branch and platform lay to the left of the station building, with the goods yard beyond.
Tim Shuttleworth

The section between Falk's Junction and the Meadow (South) Works was taken out of use on 1st May, 1965, and rail traffic finally ceased on the remainder of the branch between Winsford Junction and the West (Meadowbank and Falk's) Works as from 13th March, 1967. Latterly the only traffic had been to the Rock Mine. The branch officially closed on 5th June, 1967 and Winsford Junction signal box was abolished on 11th February, 1968. It is not known if any diesel locomotives operated on the branch in its last days; Northwich Shed remained in use for steam engines until March 1968 so the Winsford and Over branch could well have remained steam worked right to the end. One main line diesel did traverse most of the branch after closure however, when a class '40' locomotive ventured in the Spring of 1968 as far as a point close to Wade's Crossing, evidently to protect British Rail's interest when work on a new road connection to a sewage works was being carried out by Winsford Council. Also the trains used for the recovery of the track will have been diesel hauled.

After closure some 5½ miles of the trackbed were purchased on 26th March, 1969 by the Cheshire County Council for conversion into a footpath and bridleway, or what at the time was termed a linear park. The Council's portion commences just south of Winsford Junction, access here being discouraged but is possible via Waste Lane, and continues right through to Falk's Junction, then follows the branch to the West Works as far as the level crossing with New Road. Whitegate station building, platform and one nameboard (turned to face the opposing direction) still stand, remarkably little altered. This is the main access point, the footpath being called 'Whitegate Way', and the goods yard has been turned into a car park with picnic tables and toilet facilities.

Two of the overbridges between Whitegate and Catsclough have been removed and pedestrians, as well as horses, have to come down off the embankment, cross the road on the level, and then climb up on the embankment again on the other side at both these places. At Catsclough Crossing the gatekeeper's house, a standard CLC building although somewhat altered, is still occupied; the level crossing gates are also still in position and there is even a short length of track in the road. The nameboard off the little signal cabin is fixed to the fence in front of the house. South of Falk's Junction all the once numerous salt works have been demolished, much of the trackbed has disappeared and as one nears Winsford it becomes increasingly difficult to tell there was once a railway here at all. There is no sign of the several siding connections that used to cross the road to enter the salt works. At the terminus the goods shed and the station cottages had been demolished by March 1960 although the former passenger buildings were then still intact. Today all trace of the station has gone. There are still the signalmen's cottages at Winsford Junction whilst Cuddington station remains largely unaltered and in good order, as do the cottages on the Warrington Road.

Principal Officers of the Cheshire Lines Committee

Secretary

1863-1892 Edward Ross
1892-1922 Glegge Thomas
1922-1925 John E. Charnley
1925-1926 W. Howard Oates
1926-1935 T.R. Smith
1936-1947 Gerald Leedham

Manager

1863-1882 William English
1882-1904 David Meldrum
1904-1910 James Pinion
1910-1925 John E. Charnley
1925-1926 W. Howard Oates
1926-1929 Alfred P. Ross
1929-1932 Sydney T. Burgoyne
1933-1947 Gerald Leedham

Engineer

1863-1865 John S. Wilkinson
1866-1874 Charles R. Sacré
1875-1902 W. George Scott
1902-1917 Harry Blundell
1917-1929 Alfred P. Ross
1929-1936 K.C. Marrian
1936-1947 (LMS office)

Accountant

1867-1896 R.R. Walker
1896-1922 Jonathan Young
1923-1928 James Mohan
1928-1936 K. W. Doughty
1936-1947 (LMS office)

Stores Superintendent

1880-1887 W. Henry Legge
1888-1921 S. Saxon Barton
1922-1933 J.F. Frappell
1933-1947 (LNER/LMS joint office)

Surveyor & Land Agent

1878-1922 Glegge Thomas
1922-1923 James W. Oldham
1923-1935 A.J. Brickwell
1935-1936 H.W.J. Powell
1936-1947 (LMS office)

Appendix Two

Extracts from the 1870 Inspection Report

The branch is 6 miles 5 chains long and is single throughout, excepting at Whitegate and Winsford stations where there are sidings; but the land has been purchased and all the works except earthworks and one underbridge have been constructed for a double line . . . The steepest gradient has an inclination of 1 in 80 and the sharpest curve a radius of 10 chains. The depth of the deepest cutting is 32 feet and the height of the highest embankment 37 feet.

There are four bridges over the line variously constructed of masonry in combination with cast or wrought iron girders, the largest span being 37 feet. The underbridges are five in number, one built entirely of brickwork, four have brick abutments spanned by cast iron girders, the largest of these openings being 39 feet . . . The ballast at present on the line is very sandy, but the Engineer states that it is the intention to substitute ashes for it by degrees. The fencing in some cases is post and rail, in others iron bar.

When the Bill for the latter portion of the line was before Parliament in 1867, a road at 4 m. 57 ch. (*Catsclough Crossing*) was scheduled as an occupation road, and two others at 5 m. 30 ch. (*Wade's Crossing*) and 5 m. 65 ch. (*Baker's Lane*) as public roads. Colonel Yolland reported against the latter two being crossed on the level, but the Lords' Committee decided that they might be.

In the returns now submitted by the Engineer, the road at 4 m. 57 ch. . . . is stated to be a parish road; it has been crossed on the level and the crossing provided with ordinary public road level crossing gates, lodge and signals. The roads at 5 m. 30 ch. and 5 m. 65 ch. . . . are now stated to be occupation roads - the former has been provided with gates which close across the line, signals and a warden hut; the latter with simply ordinary occupation gates. I have written to the Clerk of the East Eddisbury Highways Board, which I understand has jurisdiction over these roads, to try to ascertain what they really are. I had hoped to meet him here when I inspected the line, but he did not meet me, nor have I got an answer to my letter.

I am informed that the line is to be worked by Train Staff and Ticket, and that the passenger trains are to be booked from Northwich to Winsford and back, at both of which stations there are engine turntables . . . The only points on the line requiring attention or alteration are the supplying of two connecting rods to the points at Winsford Junction, altering a siding signal at Winsford station, and improving the working of some level crossing gates.

Lt Colonel C.S. Hutchinson, RE,
for the Board of Trade

Opening Times of Signal Boxes

	Winsford Junction	Whitegate	Falk's Junction Wade's Crossing Winsford
1892	Mon-Sat 6.00 am to 9.00 pm	Mon-Sat 8.00 am to 8.00 pm	Mon-Sat 6.00 am to 9.00 pm
1899	Mon-Sat 6.30 am to LBT (8.28 pm)	Mon-Sat 8.30 am to 8.10 pm	Mon-Sat 6.30 am to 9.30 pm
1906	Mon-Sat 6.30 am to LBT (8.28 pm)	Mon-Sat 8.15 am to 8.10 pm	Mon-Sat 6.00 am to 9.30 pm
1918	Mon-Sat 4.45 am to LBT (10.55 pm) Sunday 7.00 am to LBT (6.54 pm)	Mon-Fri 10.00 am to 8.00 pm Saturday 7.00 am to 5.00 pm	Mon-Sat 4.30 am to 11.30 pm Sunday 7.00 am to LBT (7.10 pm)
1928	Mon-Fri 6.00 am to 10.00 pm Saturday 6.00 am to LBT (10.58 pm)	Not given (closed as a block post by 1921)	Mon-Fri 6.15 am to 10.00 pm Saturday 6.15 am to LBT (11.12 pm)

LBT = After the passing of the Last Branch Train (time of train given in brackets).

Summary of Passenger Train Services

Departures from Winsford (Up): Weekdays only

	am	am	am	pm	pm	pm	pm	pm	pm	pm	pm	pm	pm
1887	-	-	*9.10	*12.15		-	*4.00	-	-	-	-	-	-
1891/92	-	8.10	9.25	12.25		-	4.10	-	5.35	-	7.20	-	-
1894	-	8.10	9.10	12.25		-	4.10	-	5.50	-	7.25	-	-
1898	-	8.10	9.25	12.20		-	4.05	-	5.50	-	7.50	-	-
1902/03	-	8.10	9.25	12.20		-	4.10	-	5.50	-	7.50	-	-
1903	-	8.15	9.25	12.20		-	4.10	SX 5.20	SO 5.50	SX 6.25	7.50	-	-
1909/10	MO 6.40	8.05	9.15	12.25		MWSO 2.15	4.15	SX 5.25	SO 5.50	SX 6.32	8.05	-	-
1914/15	MO 6.40	8.05	9.15	FX 12.20	FO †12.20	MWSO 2.15	4.15	-	SO 5.50	SX 6.32	8.05	-	-
1915	MO 6.40	8.05	9.15	FX 12.20	FO †12.20	MWSO 2.15	4.15	-	SO 5.50	SX 6.32	8.05	-	-
1917/18	-	8.05	9.22	FX 12.20	FO †12.20	-	4.10	-	6.10	-	7.35	-	-
1918/19	-	8.05	9.22	FX 12.20	FO †12.20	-	4.10	-	6.10	-	7.35	-	-
1921/1922	†6.00	7.25	9.25	SX 12.20	SO †12.20	WSO 2.15	SX +4.10	SO 4.10	6.10	-	†7.35	-	-
1922	†6.00	7.30	9.25	SX 12.20	SO †12.20	WSO 2.15	SX +4.10	SO 4.10	6.10	-	†7.35	-	SO 10.15
1925	-	7.30	9.20	SX 12.20	SO †12.20	SO 2.15	4.15	-	SO 6.05	SX 6.25	†7.35	-	SO 10.15
1927/28	-	7.30	9.20	SX 12.20	SO †12.20	SO 2.15	4.15	-	SO 6.05	SX 6.40	8.35	-	SO 10.15
1928/29	-	7.30	9.20	SX 12.20	SO †12.20	SO 2.15	4.20	-	SO 6.05	SX 6.40	8.35	-	SO 10.15
1929/30	-	7.30	9.20	SX 12.20	SO †12.20	2.15	4.20	-	SO 6.05	SX 6.35	8.35	SX +9.55	SO 10.15
1930/31	-	7.30	9.20	SX 12.20	SO †12.20	2.15	4.20	-	6.05	SX 6.35	8.35	SX +9.55	-

Departures from Cuddington (Down): Weekdays only

	am	am	am	pm	pm	pm	pm	pm	pm	pm	pm	pm
1887	–	–	*10.50	*1.10	–	*5.10	–	–	–		–	–
1891/92	–	8.40	10.50	1.00	–	4.55	–	–	6.10		8.15	–
1894	–	8.45	10.45	1.00	–	4.55	–	–	6.35		8.25	–
1898	–	8.45	10.50	1.15	–	4.55	–	–	6.45		8.25	–
1902/03	–	8.45	10.45	1.00	–	SO 4.55	SX 5.20	–	7.00		8.25	–
1903	MO 7.20	8.45	10.45	1.00	–	4.55	–	SX 6.00	7.00		8.25	–
1909/10	MO 7.20	8.40	10.45	1.00	MWSO 2.50	5.00	–	SX 5.55	7.00		8.55	–
1914/15	MO 7.20	8.45	10.45	1.00	MWSO 2.50	SO 5.00	SX 5.35	–	7.00		8.55	–
1915	MO 7.20	8.45	10.45	FX 1.15 / FO †1.15	MWSO 2.50	SO 5.00	SX 5.35	–	7.00		8.55	–
1917/18	–	8.45	11.30	FX 1.15 / FO †1.15	–	SO 5.15	SX 5.38	–	7.05		8.05	–
1918/19	–	8.45	11.30	–	WSO 3.00	SO 5.15	SX 5.38	–	7.05		8.05	–
1921/22	†6.50	8.30	10.55	SX 1.22 / SO †1.22	SO 3.00 / WSO 3.00	SO 4.55	SX †5.42	–	7.10		†9.27	–
1922	†6.49	8.30	10.55	SX 1.22 / SO †1.22	SO 3.00 / WSO 3.00	SO 4.55	SX †5.42	–	7.10		†9.32	–
1925	–	8.42	10.55	SX 1.07 / SO †1.22	MWSO 2.50 / SO 3.10	SO 4.55	SX 5.57	–	7.10	SO 7.25	†9.42	SO 10.50
1927/28	–	8.42	11.00	SX 1.07 / SO †1.22	SO 3.10	SO 5.00	SX 6.00	–	SX 7.10	SO 7.25	9.25	SO 10.55
1928/29	–	8.42	11.00	SX 1.10 / SO †1.22	SO 3.10	SO 5.00	SX 6.00	–	SX 7.10	SO 7.25	9.25	SO 10.55
1929/30	†6.57	8.42	10.55	SX 1.10 / SO †1.22	3.10	SO 5.00	SX 6.00	–	SX 7.10	SO 7.25	9.25	SO 10.55
1930/31	†6.57	8.42	10.55	SX 1.10 / SO †1.22	3.10	SO 5.00	SX 6.00	–	SX 7.10	SO 7.25	9.25	SO 10.55

* = Mixed Train   † = Train to or from Northwich   Double years (eg. 1891/92) are Winter Timetable. Single years are Summer Timetable .

Appendix Five

Summary of Goods Train Services

Departures from Winsford (Up): Weekdays only

	am 7.00	am 9.30	pm 1.00	pm 4.15	pm
1885/86	7.00	9.30	1.00	4.15	- SX
1887	6.30	*9.10	12.15	*4.00	6.15 SX
1902/03	6.30	†9.45	am #11.10	3.30	§7.35 SX
1917/18	6.00	-	11.35	3.35	#11.10 SX
1918	-	-	11.35	3.35	#7.40 SX
1928	6.45	-	11.15	SO #3.35 / SX #4.15	-
1928/29	6.45	-	11.15	SO #3.35 / SX #4.45	- SX
1931/32	-	-	#11.20	#4.00	#6.30 SX
1937/38	-	-	#11.20	#4.00	#6.30 SX
1942/43	-	-	#11.20	#4.00	#6.30 SX
1953	-	-	#12.00 SX	-	#5.25 SX
1961	-	-	#11.25	-	#3.30

Departures from Cuddington (for Winsford) (Down) (Weekdays only)

	am 8.00	am 11.00	pm 2.10	pm 5.40	pm
1885/86	8.00	11.00	2.10	5.40	- SX
1887	7.30	*10.50	*1.10	*5.10 SX	7.10 SX
1902/03	7.30	#8.32	#1.40	4.30	5.00 SX
1917/18	7.40	-	1.35	SX 5.10 / SO 5.30	8.10 SX
1918	7.40	-	1.35	SX #4.32 / SO #6.32	SX 5.12 / SO 5.30
1928	7.55	-	12.40	SX #3.15 / SO #6.32	-
1928/29	7.55	-	12.40	SX #3.15 / SO #6.32	-
1931/32	#7.55	-	#1.15 SX	#5.30	-
1937/38	#7.52	-	#1.15 SX	#5.10	-
1942/43	#7.30	-	#1.15 SX	#5.10	-
1953	#7.39	- SX	#1.30 SX	-	-
1961	-	#10.18	#1.22	-	-

† = Coal Empties to Haydock Colliery. § = Express Goods to Heaton Mersey Sidings.
* = Mixed Train. # = Train to or from Northwich.

Milepost Distances

From Manchester Central						
M.	Ch.		M.	Ch.	M.	Ch.
20	48	Northwich Station			0	00
24	78	Cuddington, Ground Frame Cabin			4	30
25	12	Cuddington Signal Box			4	44
25	16	Cuddington Station			4	48
25	68	WINSFORD JUNCTION and Signal Box	0	00		
26	42	Bridge 147, Northwich to Chester Road (A556)	0	54		
27	01	Bridge 148, Warrington to Tarporley Road (A49)	1	13		
28	05	Newchurch Crossing	2	17		
28	65	WHITEGATE STATION	2	77		
28	67	Whitegate Signal Box	2	79		
29	37	Bridge 153, Cuddington to Over Road (Marton)	3	49		
30	13	Ellis's Crossing	4	25		
30	51	Catsclough Crossing	4	63		
31	03	FALK'S JUNCTION and Signal Box	5	15	0	00
		Falk's Meadowbank Salt Works (CLC boundary)			0	26
31	26	Wade's Crossing and Signal Box	5	38		
31	29	Hickson's Salt Works Siding	5	41		
31	33	Verdin's Knight's Grange Salt Works Siding	5	45		
31	45	Deakin's Over Salt Works Siding	5	57		
31	61	Baker's Lane Crossing (occupation)	5	73		
31	64	Branch to Verdin's Meadow Salt Works	5	76	0	00
		Meadow Salt Works (CLC boundary)			0	05
31	67	Winsford Signal Box	5	79		
31	76	WINSFORD AND OVER STATION	6	08		
32	01	Hamlett's Central Salt Works (CLC boundary)	6	13		
		TOTAL LENGTH OF BRANCH: double track	0	76		
		single track	5	17		
			6	13		
		Branches to Falk's and Meadow Works (single)	0	31		
		Total	6	44		

Mileposts are positioned every 20 chains on the down side of the line.

Thanks

Finally, my thanks for help with photographs and for specialist information freely given by Trevor Booth, John Dixon and the late Geoffrey Platt (signalling), the late Guy Hemingway (contractors), Vic Bradley, Michael Cook, the late Alex Appleton, the late Bernard Roberts and the Industrial Locomotive Society (contractors' and salt works' engines), David Goodwin and the Historical Model Railway Society (rolling stock), Ron Simpson and the Manchester Locomotive Society (main line engines and railcars), Gregory Fox (estate plans), the late Peter Norton (newspaper searches), the late Harry Townley, Russell Wear, Alan Wilkinson and the Salt Museum, Northwich (the salt industry), Gordon Biddle (Weaver Navigation), Rex Christiansen, Neville Fields, Jim Peden and Tim Shuttleworth (illustrations), the Cheshire Record Office (deposited plans and other material), British Transport Historical Records (WCR and CLC minute books and other records, now housed in the Public Record Office), plus a special thank you to my wife Kaye for checking the manuscript and correcting my grammar and spelling.
And a sobering thought to finish with. If the LNWR had simply extended one of its own salt branches in the early 1860s by a bridge over the Weaver to the works on the west bank, as had been suggested, then it is most unlikely that this highly individual Cheshire Lines branch would ever have been built.

The remains of one of the gates at Wade's Crossing could still be observed as recently as July 1999. The view looking towards Falk's Junction with the site of the gatehouse in the bushes on the left.   *Author*